Confidence

The Ultimate Guide to Lead With Authenticity

(The Truth About Self-confidence and What It Really Takes to Create It)

Thomas Shumate

Published By **Tayson Maxwell**

Thomas Shumate

All Rights Reserved

Confidence: The Ultimate Guide to Lead With Authenticity (The Truth About Self-confidence and What It Really Takes to Create It)

ISBN 978-1-77485-448-8

All rights reserved. No part of this guide may be reproduced in any form without permission in writing from the publisher except in the case of brief quotations embodied in critical articles or reviews.

Legal & Disclaimer

The information contained in this book is not designed to replace or take the place of any form of medicine or professional medical advice. The information in this book has been provided for educational and entertainment purposes only.

The information contained in this book has been compiled from sources deemed reliable, and it is accurate to the best of the Author's knowledge; however, the Author cannot guarantee its accuracy and validity and cannot be held liable for any errors or omissions. Changes are periodically made to this book. You must consult your doctor or get professional medical advice before using any of the suggested remedies, techniques, or information in this book.

Upon using the information contained in this book, you agree to hold harmless the Author from and against any damages, costs, and expenses, including any legal fees potentially resulting from the application of any of the information provided by this guide. This disclaimer applies to any damages or injury caused by the use and application, whether directly or indirectly, of any advice or information presented, whether for breach of contract, tort, negligence, personal injury, criminal intent, or under any other cause of action.

You agree to accept all risks of using the information presented inside this book. You need to consult a professional medical practitioner in order to ensure you are both able and healthy enough to participate in this program.

TABLE OF CONTENTS

introduction 1

Chapter 1: What Is Confidence? 3

Chapter 2: The On/Off Switch Our Personal Potential 13

Chapter 3: Mindsets Of Confidence Both Right And Wrong 22

Chapter 4: Charisma - An Acquired Skill 33

Chapter 5: Rewarding Yourself 48

Chapter 6: The Challenge Of Overcoming Limit Belief Self-Doubt And Fear 53

Chapter 7: When Self-Confidence Gets Too Exaggerated 67

Chapter 8: Practical Strategies To Increase Confidence 75

Chapter 9: Self-Confidence Self-Fulfilling Prophecies And Virtuous/Vicious Circles 82

Chapter 10: Understanding The Importance Of Discipline 89

Chapter 11: The Foundation 99

Chapter 12: Habits You Must Follow Daily To Build And Increase Your Self-Esteem 112

Chapter 13: Strategies For On The Day Of The Event 130

Chapter 14: Acknowledge Your Fears And Successes.. 142

Chapter 15: Self Confidence Strategy -"Look The Part... 150

Chapter 16: Effective Strategies To Ensure Success 163

Chapter 17: The Common Roots Of Low Self-Esteem... 171

Conclusion 182

Introduction

Before you guys go ahead, click here to get free confidence eBooks and audiobooks

The ability to trust is crucial for your child's development during the very beginning of life. It's crucial because it's necessary to face many of the obstacles your child will encounter throughout their life. It is the obligation of the parent to support the child in building confidence in themselves. You can assist your child to build confidence in various ways.

Instilling confidence in your child's self will not only help them feel more confident about themselves, but it can aid them in preparing for their future. It is possible to ask, "What can I do to help my child develop confidence in themselves?" The answer is easy, and there are a some ways you can be doing regularly to help. They can be done in a matter of minutes.

This book will provide you with an understanding of the importance of confidence in yourself and the best way to go about accomplishing this. The process of building confidence in your child is much simpler if you pay careful to your child's needs and absorb the entire details.

Chapter 1: What Is Confidence?

"It is the confidence we have in our minds, bodies, and spirits that allow us to continue seeking exciting new experiences." Oprah Winfrey

Confidence is a concept that has been developed in the last few years but has a rooted historical origin. The term "confidence" originates from the Latin word 'confides' meaning 'with confidence'. Confidence, at its heart is the ability to trust in your own abilities and self-confidence.

Confidence is the foundation of belief.

If you're confident, you believe in your talents, abilities and capability to reach your objectives. Instead of relying on other people, you rely on your own judgement. To be sure is to be able to trust that you are 100% certain that you will be successful.

Confident thinking isn't an entirely new idea. Succession-oriented people believe that their success is due to their confidence as well as the ability and luck. The legendary athlete Michael Jordan, for example is a man who has proven the power of faith over and over again. At his high school days, Jordan was cut from the varsity team in his sophomore year. However rather than get down, he was determined and determined. Jordan continued training, train and improve his basketball skills. player. In spite of his unwavering faith in himself, he was selected for the team that year. He was able to join the University of North Carolina under an athletic scholarship. The year 1982 was his very first year in university, Jordan was named Rookie of the Year. His team was awarded the NCAA championship. After being named a college athlete of the year over the following two seasons, Jordan was selected with the Chicago Bulls in the 1984 NBA draft. He was also part of the 1984 Summer United States Olympic basketball team that took home an Olympic gold medal. The year 1993 was a different story, and Jordan was already a winner of three consecutive NBA championships in the regular season, three regular season as well as playoff MVP awards, as well as seven consecutive scoring championships.

Despite his phenomenal accomplishments, Jordan's life was changed forever in the summer of 1993, when his father was killed. In the wake of that tragedy the Jordans decided to quit professional basketball shortly after.

A man of this strength and confidence will never be dissuaded from his ambitions and Jordan returned to the NBA during the 1994-95 season following the absence of seventeen months.

The world was in doubt when his return to the pro basketball arena and his faith in his talent was greater than any doubt. After losing the playoffs during his first season, Jordan led the Bulls to their fourth NBA championship in the 1995-96 campaign. The final game took place in celebration of Father's Day, the three-year anniversary of his father's tragic murder. Since that time, Jordan went on to achieve a sixth and fifth NBA title and secure his place in the NBA history.

If Jordan was not capable of persevering spite of his personal anxiety, he might not have achieved his goal to become one of the best (if not the best) players who have ever played basketball. If he'd given up at the age of an incoming sophomore at high school, no one would have known the name of Michael Jordan is today. As I do, you are probably not blessed with the athletic abilities to be the next Michael Jordan, however, you have the innate talents that are what make you the person you are. Utilize them with confidence and trust in yourself. If you don't, no one can.

I want to make it clear that I am not proposing to take on 4 million dollars in debt. I want to be able to share his story to show that confidence is an essential element of achievement. There's no difference between the two of them He simply did what he believed and took consistent and deliberate steps to turn his dreams into reality.

How are confidence and courage In Relation?

To be confident is to be confident in your capabilities and to act on that conviction What is courage? Aren't they both the same thing?

I'm not an expert on bravery, therefore I'd like to refer to Eric Kaufmann as an outstanding speaker, author as well as a corporate trainer. Within the course of his TED Talk, Kaufmann describes his experience of quitting work and donating all of his personal possessions, creating an unfinished cabin within the forest, as well as committing himself to a spiritual practice has been a part of his life for the past 10 years. Kaufmann expected the process to be a spiritual awakening however, he didn't anticipate the intenseness with the intensity with which he would be confronting his fears. At first, he was afraid of failing, the fear that he would fall short in his professional and personal ventures. He was afraid that other people would discover that the truth about him. He was not as powerful or intelligent as they believed. The feelings eventually boiled down to a deep-seated fear was unworthy of happiness or success. Depressed and isolated and depressed, his thoughts of inadequacy took over his mind to the point where the only option was to take his own life. He recollects this idea was "truly frightening," but he survived by overcoming his fears.

Courage is, as defined by Kaufmann describes it as "deliberately moving towards things you'd rather not do." Similar to confidence the cultivation of courage is also possible and is just as in our lives as fear. In actual fact, developing relationships with your fear by using Kaufmann's method is one of the ways we can use to increase our confidence.

In his presentation He suggests three steps to overcome fear to face it: Feel, Face and Accept. Instead of trying to escape the fear, you should be able to experience it, not only by acknowledging that you're afraid, but also by being aware of the effect it has on your body as well as your spirit. Allow it to grip you and let it be present without trying to ignore it. When you are able to feel your anxiety, take a moment, the next step is to take three long breaths. When you try to put your thoughts down by allowing yourself to breathe, you allow yourself space. This allows you to have a chance to choose whether you let fear engulf your or you pursue it. If you decide to let fear go, you can confront it by naming it. Kaufmann says, "As soon as you are able to identify something, you're able to manage the issue." In lieu of letting the fear take over as your ruler it is choosing to become its companion. The last step is to face the fear and face it with the force of plans. The plan you create is not centered on conquering anxiety, but instead making it easier to deal with it. When you face the things you fear head-on and learn to control your response in fear build confidence.

A side note: my uncle Eric was not a suicide victim. He was a fantastic mentor, friend , and a beloved member to my entire family. I am thankful that I am close to an individual of his caliber and his book The Four Virtues of A Leader The Hero's Journey: Navigating through Risk to Results is a fantastic, forward-looking guide to cultivating leadership. But I digress.

Confidence is believing in your self and actions based on this belief, courage refers to taking action with determination in spite of uncertainty or fear. The confidence you have builds courage because you must be able to take action even when you'd prefer not to. I believe that in certain instances, you must to be able to make that first step towards building confidence in yourself. In the meantime, let's keep it to an egg and chicken scenario.

What is Self-Esteem?

After we've discussed the qualities of courage and confidence, how self-esteem fits into the mix? A lot of people refer to confidence and self-esteem in the same way, but they are distinct. Confidence is the confidence in your abilities and talents however, it is also particular to your skill. For example, I believe I'm a competent basketball player and I am confident in my ability of shooting balls however, I am unable to draw a picture that will help me save myself. This isn't a sign of an insecurity general, but rather the realization that I've not spent enough effort into developing my art capability.

However self-esteem is a measure of your value to the world. If you answer, "Am I a worthwhile person" with a clear "Yes," you probably have a good self-esteem, and the reverse is also true. Self-esteem isn't a variable between different skills. If you're self-confident in one aspect that you are in, then you likely aren't in the same area as it is, as Katty Kay explains that it's "a reflection of your self-image."

How do they all fit Together?

If you are aware of your worth and you trust your own courage to try new things, and believe in yourself and your capabilities You can achieve whatever you put your heart on.

Confidence is different from. Overconfidence

While a healthy dose of confidence is essential to achieve your goals throughout your life, overconfidence can be the most effective method of making the same dreams vanish in the distance.

As you gain confidence, like everything else you do, being humble is crucial. Uncertainty could lead to impulsive decision-making that could stop your road towards success at any point especially if you're an business owner. In business, you have to interact with people in a variety of roles. Being confident in your interactions with people is vital and being overconfident can be a major turnoff. The major difference between overconfidence and confidence is the former lets you to have a realistic perception of yourself and see the areas you can improve. Overconfident people tend to overestimate their abilities and are often unwilling to acknowledge that they aren't experts in everything.

In my work as an author and entrepreneur, I, for example, constantly navigate between overconfidence and confidence. I must be confident enough to share my ideas and ideas out there, and be able to endure the severe critics (of which there are plenty) and simultaneously being humble enough to accept assistance when it's provided. I attribute a substantial portion of my personal success (limited although it could be) to constructive criticism from mentors who I confidence, and I recommend that you find yourself a mentor.

Whatever the effectiveness of the guideline that is provided in this book can be for creating confidence, it's your responsibility to remain in touch with, and considerate of others throughout your journey.

Chapter 2: The On/Off Switch Our Personal Potential

What is it about certain people can get the most out of their lives than other people? What is it that makes some people able to give a powerful presentation with confidence... and others tremble at the thought of it?

Are they because they're a bit more skill and ability? Do they have the assets that other people do not?

You and I are both aware already that this isn't true in any way.

Did Mahatma Gandhi come from a mighty family which gave him self-confidence and the ability to build the foundation for a strong power base that would free India against the British?

If you think you are able to lead others, then you can be looking to achieve anything less than a managerial post. If you think that you're just an observer that's why you shouldn't want anything more than simply a front line worker.

If you are convinced that you're capable, you should expect to do well in all the tasks you take on.

If you believe that something is unattainable or that it can't be accomplished, would you act? It's unlikely.

If you were to do this then, you'd likely end the process at the point you encounter the problem.

In the end that you could have the most potential there is but you'll never be able to tap into it. In the end, you won't see the results you want. If this happens it can further strengthen the notion that it isn't possible.

That is to say the way you think, your beliefs determine the choices you make and the extent of your potential can tap. If you believe that something can be done, you'll do everything to make it happen.

You'll be able to take huge action and will persevere in doing what you need to do to reach it. In the end, you'll tap into a lot of your potential.

If, for instance, you doubt that you'll ever be able to build an enterprise that is successful then you shouldn't even try it.

If you do decide to go into business, you'll give up when the business goes down due to your preconceived notions that 'it's too difficult' or that 'I do not have the skills'.

Your Credos

When we believe something is likely to happen, we'll draw all the resources we can to back the conviction. We'll switch to our imagination, energy and resources.

Do we think that this means we'll be able to achieve exactly what we intended?

But not all the time.

A belief in possibility can allow us to create results that go above what we could do without a conviction to begin with.

In the same way you may believe that something is out of your reach, you block out the possibility of ever reaching it. It is a way to shut down your own potential.

Since self-confidence is about trusting in yourself and the things you can achieve (your abilities) the most important thing that you must work on is your own self-confidence.

You Are What You Eat Believe!

When our belief systems have a profound influence on the quality of our lives, and even our physical health, we should begin to look at whether the beliefs we hold allow us to be more successful or restrict us. If our beliefs limit us, we need to begin changing these beliefs!

The most important thing to understand is that the opinions that you have aren't necessarily truthful.

Beliefs do not have to be substantiated.

They are just beliefs, views, and generalizations we create about the world we live in.

Whatever belief you believe in regardless of how much you believe it's factual, there's always someone who holds an entirely different belief.

For them, their beliefs are equally valid to you.

Anything You Believe In is True!

While beliefs can never be 100% accurate, they are valid for those who is a believer!

Simply because what you believe can be your reality. If you believe you're stupid and you believe that you are, then you'll become dumb. If you think you are smart and you believe that, then you'll experience.

If you think you're lucky, then you'll be lucky. If you believe that the best opportunities are coming to you, it will be true for you.

Maybe Henry Ford says it best:

"Whether you believe that you are able to or that you shouldn't... regardless, you're right!"

Why is this? Our beliefs form the main filters that decide our perception of our surroundings. In any moment, you don't experience reality, you only perceive your own version of reality.

Our brains are constantly editing and distorted by what we see and hear as well as what we feel. This is the reason why two people may experience the same thing but experience it in a different way.

If, for instance, two people had a disagreement the two parties will differ on what transpired.

It's not so much that one side or the other has a lie, as both sides erase and alter the facts they have experienced, based on their own personal opinions.

Have you ever had the moment when your parents thought that your actions were unresponsible. You can do a thousand things right but they'll only recall those few times that you were deemed irresponsible. 'Aha you're doing it again!' they'll tell you.

We do the same thing to our family, friends, members, and colleagues.

Once we've made our minds that we want to adhere to a particular belief that we hold, we be prone to focus on instances when that our beliefs are accepted but fail to consider every time our beliefs are challenged.

Whatever we believe in, becomes true for us. It becomes our truth.

Keep in mind that self-confidence can be defined as "the degree to that you are confident in yourself and the things you are able to do."

If you think you're incompetent, you'll tend to concentrate on evidence that supports this... then that is true for you.

I've witnessed many occasions where a person's belief in a certain thing becomes self-fulfilling prophecy. What you believe in is an actuality. It is because you do every action that supports the belief, which in turn encourages the outcome.

Certain people I know believe that they're incompetent. They believe they are slow learners and lack the ability and ability to adapt to life.

This is why they tend to focus on the things that take them time to master. This reinforces their beliefs and keeps them from taking advantage of any opportunity to discover something new.

How were Our Beliefs Created?

How did we get the beliefs we hold in the present?

The majority of them are derived from modeling the important people in our lives - such as our teachers, parents, and even our friends.

We are prone to adopt the same beliefs as those who influenced the most in our lives.

If our parents believe they will never have a chance to be wealthy due to their family history then you will likely adopt those beliefs for yourself.

If you grew up in a household where no one graduated from school, then you likely believe that education is hard or is not necessary.

It is true that a lot of our beliefs are also derived from our experiences in the past.

Be aware that the opinions you hold are just thoughts and opinions you form regarding these experiences.

The problem is that once we forget that these are just thoughts and start to accept them as complete truths. This is when they turn into the norms that we embed in our brain and begin to influence the way we live our lives.

While certain beliefs can actually help us however, many of them restrict our abilities at the same time. For instance, beliefs such as "I'm bad at Math", 'I'm an inefficient learner I am not able to connect well with other people I am lazy or I am too old or young'.

Chapter 3: Mindsets Of Confidence Both Right And Wrong

Want to learn more

"My most difficult task has been to alter the mentality of individuals. Mindsets are a tangled game that can fool us. We see things as our minds have taught our eyes to view." Muhammad Yunus

It's impossible to look at the world with no prejudices. This is because the experiences we had growing in the past have shaped a lot about what we are able to believe and how we view things, and how we perceive what is real.

As an example, don't assume someone who was raised in a state of extreme poverty and regular emotional and sexual assault to trust in"the "goodness" in life. It's not likely to happen for the foreseeable future or until they decide to make that choice.

This brings me to an crucial and significant aspect of the way we think - our thoughts.

Perhaps you did not grow in a socially and economically difficult area but since you witnessed a wealthy friend be bankrupt within so short a time, you often think about what it would be like to be poor at the blink at a glance. When you think over it, eventually you'll think that it's going to occur to you. When you begin to believe your thoughts, you'll begin looking at ways of making your beliefs become reality.

There's a chance that you don't have any control over all the things that occur to you - such as being dismissed from work and growing up in a poverty-stricken family, and having to shut down your business due to an employee who is a criminal - but you are in control of your thoughts. Your conscious mind which determines the majority of your actions is unable to distinguish between a real-life reality and what you make up in your head. It will simply take in whatever input you offer it or permit it to enter, and will be able to effectively allow those inputs to come to occur.

The option is yours. Do you want to hold the wrong beliefs about the person you are to let the world or your experiences define your belief in yourself , or will you take action to take action? If you're looking to begin taking action

Here are a few of the bad mentalities that should be removed before you can adopt the correct ones.

PERFECTION

One of the faulty beliefs that could cause you to be unsure of yourself is that of perfection. Many people, regrettably to say, think that you're only competent only when you're flawless. While you shouldn't be sure when you frequently fail but that doesn't mean you shouldn't be allowed to fail at times.

Perfectionists are a guaranteed recipe to suck confidence from you each time. Why? Because no one is perfect. If you're only confident in yourself only when you're completely perfect, then I have some bad news for you. You'll never feel confident.

If you imagine masculine, confident males like Michael Jordan and Novak Djokovic There's a problem: they're not the perfect athletes! If you're able to remember (or search on Google), Michael Jordan at times failed to be a part of the varsity team at his school. Many times throughout his career also, he failed shots to the floor and free shot shots. Did this affect his faith in himself and his capabilities? No.

Actually, it motivated him to continue improving on what's considered to be the greatest basketball abilities of his time.

When you think about Novak Djokovic, the world's best-ranked tennis player for men at the moment You'll notice the fact that he's not won all his games. He's also missed shots and is still doing occasionally. He's the best, however he's not completely perfect. Although he's not perfect, confident in his capability to perform at highest levels doesn't seem to be affected in any way.

MINDSETS DO NOT END.

A lot of people believe in the power of destiny - that their fates were written on the stars a some time long ago. This is why it has the following excuses:

"This is the way God created me."

"I was born into a family of poverty and will probably die in one."

"This is me and I have no say to change it!"

"Once shy always shy!"

These statements reflect the idea that everything that happens in life is permanent and cannot be modified. This isn't a good thing. Evidently, it doesn't give you any hope of an improved future, i.e. that you'll actually be confident and be an Alpha! If you didn't have this belief then you'll never accomplish the things necessary to become confident, thinking they'd just be a wasted effort.

If this is the mental which you hold dear to you and you are adamant about it, you'll avoid any task that requires the effort of changing your behavior to a better way. You could try it for a couple of days, weeks, or months, but eventually you'll fall back to the ground of your original belief that you are hopeless.

ACHIEVEMENTS = CONFIDENCE

Although it's true that successes can definitely make a people feel confident, or turn a somewhat confident person into an extremely confident man however, that doesn't mean you must first achieve to be confident. Indeed, many successful men achieved their success by believing in their own self-confidence first. Anything that isn't based on confidence in yourself is most likely incidental or a result of circumstance. For instance, a shy person who was put in a position where in which he needed to save an infant drowning. After he has succeeded the man receives such applause and adulation from the general public that it makes him feel more confident. The confidence he has gained is entirely coincidental and is likely to be only temporary, i.e., will disappear once the initial public excitement about what he's accomplished has gone.

Look at other players like LeBron James and Kobe Bryant, both of who are basketball's most famous stars who made it to the pro ranks straight out of highschool. They were so confident in their abilities that they took on the risk of transferring straight into the NBA the toughest basketball organization, and show their high school level stuff. This confidence resulted in their greatest successes - championship trophies MVP awards and more. And not the reverse.

When you're feeling that you must first achieve to build confidence do not dwell on it. You'll have to feel confident in yourself before you'll be able to accomplish anything meaningful or important.

UPROOTING MINDSETS

There are a variety of methods to get rid of negative mindsets Some are easy and cost nothing, and others are more complex and expensive. I'll give you some practical ways to eliminate the negative mental habits that prevent you from becoming more confident and turning into an alpha.

Starve The Beast

One of the best methods to take on a formidable living foe is to be able to starve it to death. All living things will die in the natural way if it is not fed and drinks. Mental states are similar to this that if you stop feeding it, the animal will die or taken away.

What ways can you feed your mind-sets? One method is to loop them through your mind. You might say "Hey I don't have to do lotus poses and chant those naive thoughts as a negative yoga instructor." Trust me it's not necessary to sign up for the yoga or meditation classes and sing "ohm Ohhh, ohm" for hours to be meditative.

If you constantly think about the reasons you aren't certain and you're not sure, you're circulating these thoughts through your head. Meditating simply means thinking about or thinking about something frequently. That's it. No matter what it is "ohm Ohm, Ohm, Ohm" or "What makes me believe I could be wealthy and successful even though I do not possess the proper connections or I'm not born into a wealthy household?", you're meditating.

The more you don't think about your bad habits and the more you stifle it. As time passes, you'll starve enough to totally eradicate or remove it.

Self-Interrogation

One of the most effective ways to slowly dismantle wrong thinking is to challenge it as well as one of the most effective methods is to continually examine its legitimacy and benefits (if it has any). Consider it as a court proceeding in which an attorney representing the defense - which is you simply tries to create an absence of reasonable doubt about the claims by the lawyer who is prosecuting, based on the incorrect mindset, and by doing so, eliminate any legal claims or authority that it might have over you. Let me clarify.

Let's look at the incorrect mindset of permanentity for instance. One method to prove the reasonable doubt is to question it in terms of its validity as well as the benefits. A few questions you could consider asking yourself about this belief include:

"How do you know this is true? What do you think of my buddy Hubert who was once convinced that there is no God? If beliefs are indeed forever and enduring, then why is he serving as a minister in a local church?"

"Will believe that I cannot change the way I feel and think about myself benefit or be detrimental to me? Do I have the ability to live my life to the fullest and achieve my ultimate goal, should I continue to believe that this is the case?"

"If I'm right that I have to accomplish something substantial before satisfied with my own abilities, what can I think of my most trusted friend George? He's not the most well-off of people did not go to college , nor is he an incarnation that of James Dean but how was it that he felt confident of contacting beautiful women across the globe and obtaining their numbers before even making his first success?"

"Would the quality of my life much better if I tossed out my current mindset that I have to be a success-oriented person first before I can be confident in myself? If I hold the faulty idea, will I be able to live my life to the fullest?"

Repeat this process often and in time, you'll find yourself slowly removing your faulty attitudes about confidence and eventually removing them completely to seed new confidence-based mental models.

Birds flock together with the same feathers. Birds

If you think the previous two strategies are too difficult for you, you could try being around confident people. There's a phenomenon known as a transference of spirits, and by being around people who are confident it is possible to get enough of the confidence virus that it can eradicate your old, negative mental attitudes.

The best teachers are those who have experience according to the old saying. The best experience is, of course, one that is personal. However, other people's experiences are also excellent instructors, helping you to get rid of the worst attitudes with little effort. There is a saying that in the process of learning, it's more about being learnt than is. Also, the action speaks louder than words. When you surround yourself with confidence-driven people You put yourself in a position to be able to see the pitfalls of your faulty confidence beliefs and slowly train your brain to remove them.

Chapter 4: Charisma - An Acquired Skill

Learn more about text chemistry free.

What is it that you need to do to be a charismatic individual? It's not enough to be aware that it is a skill that can be acquired You must also learn how to master this ability. In truth there isn't a universal formula that would make it too simple. There are some essential characteristics that charismatic people have , and these traits are listed here, so that you can sketch out a mental model of what you can like to see in a charismatic individual.

Check out the following tips and discover about the essential elements that make a charismatic individual. However it is important to understand that the primary characteristics of charisma include the capacity to be natural as well as the capacity to be confident in yourself, no matter whatever. If you are able to concentrate on developing or even (initially) to understand these two qualities then you're on the right track. To the other side, you can draw inspiration and direction from the elements listed below.

10 Essential Qualities to Develop

Are you looking for ways to become a person who is charismatic? Here are the characteristics you must work on to instill this trait within you. The more you concentrate on these traits and work to incorporate them into your daily life and your life, the more charming you'll be. The ability you'll need to develop as time passes.

1. Be natural

A charismatic person is able to be proud of who they are. There is no pretense to the charismatic person. He loves to show who he is the way he is. Take it or take it away. It is because people who are charismatic are able to accept themselves for who they are. The first and most important thing is.

It is essential to accept yourself how you are, the positive and negative. Everyone is not perfect, and every person has a certain imperfections. You must take the good and bad with each other, be yourself, accept yourself and be who you are.

If you aren't in tune with your identity it is impossible to know that others will appreciate the person you are and it's not possible to constantly play the game to gain the trust of those you love. They must love the person you are and that , you must be the person you are.

2. Be Prepared To Share Knowledge

A person who is charismatic is eager to share the things he has learned, and share details whenever necessary and feel elated when you have the chance to share something he has learned to other people. This way you'll see people who come to you for help and would be eager to discuss what they have learned with you. This is a mutual learning route.

3. Be Ready To Learn

The most charismatic people are humble, and willing to take on new challenges. There's no one who is too small to giving him a lesson. A person with charisma is always seeking information in all he does and everywhere you go. He is a constant researcher of information. Like you must be prepared to share the things you are knowledgeable about and are able to share with other people what you don't have the knowledge of. This is not just going to keep you humble, but it will also will make you attractive to people who follow and know you.

4. Be Gracious In Defeat

There are times when you win and then lose some. It's not likely that you will win every single time, just as it's impossible to lose every single time. But the way you behave whether you lose or win is what will show your character, especially when you lose.

If you want to be a person of charisma must be kind and gracious, and also congratulate the winner. Additionally, you should never use an unjust strategy or use of subterfuge to be successful. If you do you may win, but you will lose some respect among your team and that's the worst thing that could happen.

5. Be a good person in every aspect of Your Life

Charity and kindness should be a part of your everyday life. Although it is true that many charismatic leaders can't be described as kind or charitable but you should cultivate and maintain these qualities. In addition, you should be generous in your forgiveness.

It's true that some charismatic leaders in the past were charitable or generous however, that does not eliminate this particular characteristic. Someone who is charismatic feels it's his obligation to assist less fortunate people It isn't required to do so financially, but emotionally and spiritually too.

6. Be genuinely warm

A person who is charismatic is warm and friendly. To be a person who reflects these qualities, you have to be genuine as well as genuinely interested in others and humble. You need to be in the midst of people and not in a secluded area by yourself. In addition, you must be patient, understanding and truthful in all that you say and do.

The ability to be warm and friendly is an essential quality. People should be able and confident and not be judging in your listening. This is one of the traits that makes an affable person.

7. Make a Difference

A person who is charismatic can be expected to take decisive decisions whenever the need arises. Making decisions is an crucial aspect of a person's daily life. There are a few who can make a statement but the majority are the ones that you must be taking every day. You should be perceived as a shrewd person, not someone who is prone to a shaky posture every whenever there's a need to be.

This is one of the reasons why the most charismatic people enjoy a following. They are the leaders of their generation or are leaders in making.

8. Be adroit in your communication

People who are charismatic have a clear and articulate voice, and they communicate with conviction. They believe even if you don't know enough about the person to be able to trust him. You believe because he talks with complete conviction, and right directly from his heart. Each word he speaks about will keep it 100. One of the most appealing traits of a charismatic personality is the manner in which he speaks.

If he makes a statement will be a message into the soul. It is the truth and you are sure that he will be true to his word, no matter the circumstances.

Reveal Your Weaknesses

Many people are prone to downplay their weaknesses or conceal them from their peers, so that someone else would profit from the situation. This is not the case with the charismatic. People who are charismatic tend to be open about his shortcomings, honest about them, and is without apologies. The fact that he acknowledges his imperfections as they are and they are being overcome them is motivating to say the least.

Many people do not recognize the weaknesses or flaws but they do see the courage to admit the imperfections. Your weak point now becomes your strength.

Five Tools to Build Your Charisma

As previously mentioned charisma is a talent and, like all skills that can be learned and developed. For a faster way to achieve it you should consider employing a few tools.

the power of Positive Affirmations

I can accomplish this. It seems like a simple sentence, doesn't it? It's a straightforward phrase, however it's very powerful. When you encounter a challenge and you are faced with a problem, speak this out loud to yourself. Do this with conviction and faith. You will discover that, indeed you can achieve anything you want to do.

The charismatic people have a great self-esteem. They also, through their charisma they motivate others to push themselves to realize their potential to the fullest extent. Discover positive affirmations to boost confidence in yourself and increase your self-confidence and charisma.

The Effects of Body Language

Language is the body form of communication that is not deceiving. It is essential to master not only understand it correctly however, you must also to be aware of what you are displaying. Although it's extremely difficult to manage and control body language, it's simple to realize how crucial it is to understand and utilize the appropriate body language and posture when communicating with others.

People who are charismatic are usually exceptional at communicating. But mastering body language can give you an advantage.

Power of Passion Power of Passion

It is impossible to be an enthralling person unless you've got an interest. Your passion is what generates the charisma in you. It is essential to discover your passion since it is the passion you have that provides you with the drive, direction, and determination to continue moving forward regardless of any obstacles.

There is no doubt that the most successful persons are motivated by an insatiable passion that is infectious.

Power of Knowledge Power of Knowledge

The charismatic people are aware of what they're talking about and won't even speak about it. Most of the time they are the top authorities in their field of interest. They are educated and are always eager to learn more. They are people are willing to listen to anyone and everyone with something to say about the subject they are interested in with great attention.

They'll never shy away to seek out knowledge from any sources, regardless of how strange. With their humble nature they'll recognize that what they have learned can always be improved.

Think Powerfully Outside of the Box

The charismatic people never stop because of a lack of options. If something seems to be impossible for them, they'll find ways out of the box approach. The ability to solve problems by using creative and innovative techniques is a characteristic of most people who have charisma. This is the reason why a majority of people are considered to be leaders in their fields.

Nothing can stop them. Every time obstacles arise they will discover a way to overcome it. This is a technique that must be cultivated and refined to ensure that it can respond quickly in times of need.

Keep Eye Contact

The ability to make eye contact with a person is mark of confidence. People are prone to are more likely to trust people who can create and keep eye contact while speaking. The most charismatic people are adept at the art of keeping a non-threatening and not snarky eye contact when speaking to their listeners.

It's a matter of practicing to make sure you use the correct type of eye contact, or you could end up with unfavorable outcomes. Being too rigid and fixed could be perceived as intimidating. Too long and it will be perceived as flirty, too small and it could be seen as insincere. To convey trust and friendliness, you must gaze at the person in the eye for approximately 3-4 seconds prior to moving on to the next people. But, if you're talking to a single person, more time spent looking at them are beneficial.

Do be diplomatic and tactful.

The people who are charismatic do not lash headless people. They're patient, and they strive to see the different aspect on the other side. But, when they realize that their approach is the most effective they are able to are able to believe in their beliefs and have the courage to stand behind their beliefs.

When they do they can be able to say "No" in the most comfortable manner. The most charismatic people have perfected the art diplomacy. They will be able to communicate and defend their point of view without harming or offending or causing offense to the other groups of people.

Do improve your sense of Humor

Humor is among the most important tools for an affable person. A capacity to laugh at difficult and awkward situations makes a person likable to everyone. A capacity to laugh yourself is among the most appealing qualities for it shows that one is prone to mistakes and, therefore is one of the most attractive.

People who are people who are charismatic have a smile that doesn't hurt anyone, and brings a smile to one's face even in the most challenging situations.

Do be patient

It's very rare to witness someone who is charismatic loses his temper. The trait of patience is among the traits that are most appreciated not just by leaders but also in people who are charismatic. Charisma in a sense is a person you are at ease regardless of what. The ability to let others develop to their fullest potential without judgement is a great quality and the most sought-after quality.

Charisma The Don'ts

Do not show superiority

People who are charismatic attract they attract people due to their manner of speaking and act. In essence everyone who is charismatic is famous; some are in smaller circles, and others in larger circles. At no time is it likely that a person with charisma be a negative person towards anyone.

In contrast, they are accessible and humble because it is their humility that keeps them growing and developing into a better individual.

Do not be focused on self.

A charismatic person is attracted to them as they seem to be genuine curious about other people. They do not dwell on their own achievements but rather, they stay away when attention is drawn to them. They prefer to highlight the other's strengths over their own, and usually acknowledge the team , rather than them for any accomplishments achieved.

This is among the most impressive and appealing traits of a leader which is what charismatic leaders have.

Don't Talk Do the Talk

Consider what makes you so enthralled by the charismatic personalities. It's because they live up to what they claim to do. They practice what they preach. They are adamant about what they say and follow through with the principles they teach. They motivate people through action and not just through words. If a charismatic speaker speaks, they build confidence in others and encourage them to take follow their actions by the example they set.

Do not abuse People's Trust

Unfortunately, there are far too many scammers out there who appear as charming as they can be. They gain trust from people them and make use of their gullibility to deceive them. If you go back, there are plenty of instances to fill a book. A con man that was immortalized on silver screen is Frank Abagnale. The film "Catch me if you Are Able" was inspired by his life. He was a charming character and his charismatic personality enabled him to attract people who were later duped. Being a charismatic personality you know that trust is at the heart of your interactions therefore, don't overuse it!

Don't be Judicative

The people who are charismatic know that there always are two sides of an eagle. They do not judge people based on their previous mistakes. Instead, they encourage people to focus on to put their past behind them and laying their future on new ground.

They are kind, non-judgmental they are patient, kind and always ready to assist. They are truly attracted to every person that they come across and have the ability and willing to disagree with someone without making them feel like they are a burden or being offended.

Chapter 5: Rewarding Yourself

"When you are confident you'll be able to have lots of fun. If you're having fun, you can accomplish incredible things." Joe Namath. Joe Namath

The benefits of reinvesting your Successes

Congratulations! You've achieved your goal! You've accomplished something to enhance your life and you're feeling euphoric over your accomplishment. So, what can you do to boost this feeling of success and motivate yourself to achieve even greater satisfaction throughout your day? One of the most effective methods to motivate yourself to continue setting goals, whether small or big and small, is to reward yourself with an incentive when you achieve your target with success.

It may sound a bit naive or unselfish However, it's actually a proven method to keep yourself focused on becoming more successful. Because you've now learned the fact that self-confidence is tied to success, you have to understand that anything that inspires you to achieve more can also boost your confidence to increase more. Award-winning author Gretchin Rubin speaks about the fact that you can reward yourself for your efforts is something that everybody does without knowing (Rubin 2014). It's about time to acknowledge the fact that you reward yourself, you are deserving of a reward for your accomplishments and they can be useful to help you achieve more and increase your confidence to the next level.

What is a SELF-REWARD?

When we hear about rewards, we think of those fleeting delights, like an extra bite of dessert following dinner, a brand new item that we've been wanting or some other indulgence that's expensive or not connected with our regular healthy, regular behavior. However, this need not be the case as the reward you receive could be any thing you like.

If you discover that you are enjoying the videos you watch on YouTube as well as walking or chatting to your family, cleaning fresh scents, cleaning or just about everything else, you could take advantage of that as a reward. The rewards you offer yourself should be something that you are able to enjoy. If you do things you enjoy each day, then you can say that you enjoy the activity and think of it as an incentive for your daily goals-oriented actions. It is also possible to choose the small tasks you can do for yourself once you've achieved the daily goal or your weekly goals and long-term goals.

This is not harmful to your goals

Whatever you decide to do, don't give yourself anything that could hinder the ability of you to reach your objectives! If you're trying to improve your confidence, do not reward yourself with things that hinder confidence-building. If you're trying to lose weight, do not give yourself an entire week off from your diet and exercise plan. Each action you take has an effect on your final outcomes and so ensure that you're not pushing yourself further from your goal by rewarding yourself!

The purpose behind self-reward is to inspire you to push yourself to achieve and do more. It's a way to encourage you to be positive about moving forward in your daily life. Select a few ways to give yourself a reward that adheres to the guidelines above.
Verbal Rewards

EXERCISE 3:

To assist you in learning to be a better person, create an easy reward for something that you've done recently. It's essential to be accustomed to allowing the little things that you like to do as rewards for your achievements and this can aid in motivating you to achieve further successes.

To motivate self-rewards Try this exercise:

Think of something you did today that was success. Now, think about things you've done that require improvement or didn't work even if you tried. If you're unable to come up with anything in this short time then think about the past month, however don't look farther back than that.

Recognize your accomplishment and shortcomings as they are. If you feel it will help you, then say your story loudly about what you accomplished with success and what failed.

Offer yourself praise verbally when you're your success. If it's appropriateto do so, select physical rewards as well to provide yourself with a motivational source to help you achieve your goals daily.

Take a look at your mistake and think about what you could be able to accomplish next time, to increase your odds of succeeding. Don't be critical of yourself for your mistakes, as this could reduce your confidence and reduce your confidence in your abilities. Make your mistakes into lessons and tell yourself "I will do better next time, to ensure I achieve my goals. This is the second issue that doesn't work for me, and I'm going to avoid making this error again in the future."

Rewarding yourself motivates you to keep making progress even greater. The greater your success greater your levels of confidence will increase. If you are looking to boost confidence in yourself ensure that you are providing yourself with the appropriate rewards for every achievement you achieve!

What to take away

If you give yourself a reward for even small successes throughout your life, you're instilling more positive behaviors that help you reach your goals in life and move to a higher degree of confidence. Learn from your mistakes and celebrate your achievements if you're looking to build confidence.

Chapter 6: The Challenge Of Overcoming Limit

Belief Self-Doubt And Fear

1. Overcoming limit belief

Our beliefs determine and guide our actions, and a lot of people believe that it's external influences that determine their lives. In reality, all personal changes begin with beliefs instead of the behavior that some consider it to be.

You will be taught how to identify your beliefs that are limiting you to determine the root of the problem determine what objective you'd like to accomplish in the event of a moment of mental blockage, then change the old belief, and then reinforce it until it is the norm.

In the end, what exactly is a limiting or limitative belief? It's the kind of idea, belief or idea that prevents us from taking the actions which could yield positive outcomes for our life.

Although the word may seem to resemble something spiritually but it doesn't mean anything in the sense of. The word "belief" refers to something that we consider to be true every fibre that make up our existence.

The majority of our beliefs were born from our experiences as we were still developing the system that would inform us about the significance of each experience at the time we formed our personal sources. Our beliefs define the things we think about throughout our lives.

As children For instance there were no sources to base our decisions on alone, and so the our family members, friends and teachers parents, friends and even our schoolmates directly influenced our behavior and thinking.

Media and society can also be blamed for us coming up with many limiting and undefined concepts. Think about a few notions you believed in but that now aren't logical...

Thus, our beliefs were constructed without conscious thought because often we were not able to stop and question the beliefs we held. This is how we've grown up without realizing the negative consequences certain beliefs have been able to have on our lives.

The belief state is the mental state that is when a person believes in absolute certainty that something is real (even when it doesn't have anything to do with the reality of it all). In this state , it sends out congruous messages to our brain making it clear that there is no doubt. In the event that you trust in the possibilities and possibilities, that's what you'll find when you travel. If you are a believer in limitations then your life suddenly is a blur and you lose focus.

We have many people who delay their actions because they think they'll never achieve their desired goals.

Due to our need for certainty, we usually want belief that we are true. The majority of our beliefs are linked to:

Money

People

Opportunities

Learning

Capabilities

Identity

Situations

Time

Life

Past, Present , Future

Methods to conquer any kind of doubt that's preventing you from achieving any sort of goal, professionally or personally.

Step 1 - Determine Which Limiting Beliefs Stop you from taking action

The first step to overcome the negative beliefs that limit you is to determine what beliefs hinder you. The most efficient method to accomplish this is to grab the pen and paper and record them on.

Step 2: Determine the Root of the Limiting Belief

Locating the source of the limitation of belief is to determine what circumstances in your life caused where the belief was created. Finding the root cause could be extremely helpful in understanding the feelings that arise from a circumstances that stop a person from advancing his life.

The goal of determining the reason is simply to examine the circumstances that we encounter in our lives, where we come up with "confusing thoughts," not to justify our present behavior. We don't want be able to attribute the previous events and we need to know the point at which that the thought was formed and then alter the way we think about it. The goal is to come up with an answer and not more.

A lot of the beliefs that limit us were engrained in us as children as we began to build our perceptions of different aspects of life.

We learn, hear and play around with concepts that do not seem to make sense when we are adults. Recognizing the root of our limiting beliefs is already a sign of the things we need to change.

How can you determine the source? Most of the time, our beliefs are tied to the past. People can recall clearly the day they came up with the belief that keeps them from doing something important that they want to accomplish in their daily lives.

Critique, embarrassing moments and traumatic incidents, as well as stories that our grandparents told us Any notion that is imposed on or offered to us might have developed into an idea that is restrictive.

Utilize your imagination and determination to determine what is the root of the belief that prevents you from taking action now. Consider this... When you're struggling with something that stops you from moving forward It means that you're looking to accomplish an objective but feel stuck.

Step 3 - Determine what goals you're trying to reach

We encounter limiting beliefs at the time we set our sights on a goal and, for some reason, we start to undermine ourselves by believing that we won't be able to achieve it. Certain people are not able to manage their emotions.

It is commonplace for us to have a desire while at the same we turn to us and ask:

I can't do this!

I'm not able to do it!

I don't know what to do!

These assertions can affect our actions when we are led to believe that we can't accomplish anything. The solution is to identify the objective you'd like to reach.

A clear objective is crucial to guide our resources and our capabilities towards the direction we wish to go, and not to what we think we're unable to achieve.

This way it will help us focus on our goals, not focusing on what we are limiting ourselves to. By doing this, we stand a the best chance to overcome harmful emotions.

Ask yourself questions like: "What do I want to accomplish in this particular situation? What is my objective? You'll be amazed to be able to answer this question.

We often think that we aren't able to accomplish something without knowing precisely what we're looking for... Do you have any experience with this? It's easier to identify our goals and the emotional hurdles we have to conquer instead of saying "I am not able or I cannot."

If you choose to do this and make it a priority, you've achieved a lot in your personal life, freeing yourself from the emotional chains that prevent you from discovering the person you truly are. Many people set goals but fail to replace their negative beliefs with positive ones.

Step 4 : Replace Limiting Belief by an empowering belief

Our beliefs are the main driver behind our behavior The most efficient method to achieve congruous and long-lasting change is to replace old and unhelpful beliefs with new ones.

It is a known fact that certain sufferers are so enslaved to destructive behavior that they can not want to accept innovative ideas or different methods of thinking.

The first thing to do is that you must be willing to change as no technique course, idea, or knowledge will alter people. The individual must take the decision to change their lifestyle and live a healthier, more successful life. In this way the strategies and concepts will be more efficient when it comes to the process.

In this process we'll replace the negative belief with a stronger belief. How do we do it? There are many of methods, but I'll present the one I have found to be the most efficient and speediest one: asking questions.

There are many questions we can ask that make us question our beliefs. Perhaps we are in a circumstances that force us to do something we thought we were unable to do.

One of the most efficient method to accomplish this is to write down your old beliefs on paper , and then develop new beliefs that empower you.

A simple action can transform your life. We often get to this point , but we don't see any progress. What happens is that people buck their convictions and forget to make them an habit. On this topic, this is the next subject.

Step 5 - Condense the new belief until it is a Habit

Our beliefs can influence our behavior without conscious thought. A belief is a conviction as soon as we do not doubt it in any way.

For instance, we are aware that skies are blue and there is no need reminders of the fact that it is blue. Once we have reached the point of belief, as well as "know" that there is a truth that we are in a state of autopilot.

And what is this got to have to do with conditioning a new conviction? All! Imagine that you create a new type of belief and continue to use it continuously? You'll begin to believe without thinking about. In reality, you'll be able to carry out this behavior normally with no pain or suffering, as was the case previously.

The process of conditioning the new belief involves creating the ideal reality for yourself within your mind by visualizing the desired outcome you would like to attain. Visualization is a fantastic method to build anticipation since you're experiencing the outcome you wish to attain.

This way, you'll be sending the right messages to the brain which makes it work for your benefit.

Listen, see and feel the desired outcome you'd like to attain in your mind. Perform this exercise each day for at least 5 minutes. You will be amazed at the results from this simple exercise bring to your daily life. You can easily get rid of any negative beliefs that stop you from moving forward.

2. Believe in your own strength and confidence

"Love is able to ward off fear, and fear, in turn, is the cause of love being snuffed out. Not only love is fear a factor in driving away as well as the goodness of humanity, intelligence, and any thoughts of beauty or truth. Only mute despair remains. And in the end, fear is able to separate mankind from the human race. "

Aldous Huxley

If you're like the majority of people, you've got an objective or a vision which is extremely important to you and you'd like to achieve it. The goal may be connected to to personal development, like losing weight, gaining self-esteem and the quest for inner peace, boost your energy levels or get over depression.

Your goal could be to return to school, establish your own business, or showcase your talents to a larger public. The process of setting goals is the easy part. The challenge of overcoming your own personal obstacles could be a nightmare, or completely awestruck by the fear you have created.

If you've tried to accomplish your goals, but ended up stopping because of an obstacle that seemed insurmountable Do not quit. This is a fact of how you approach objectives. They will take you to new place and you are faces to face with your own doubts and fears. The question isn't about how to conquer the fear, but instead making positive choices that boost your confidence, even the presence of fear.

Everyday, many people quit their dream because of fear and doubt. But it shouldn't be that way! Here are six ways to get over doubt, conquer fear and accomplish your goals in your life.

1. Make a decision.

Once you've defined your goal or dream then decide what you'd like to accomplish and be happy with it. It might seem simple however, many people do not take the plunge to commit 100% to their goal. They just continue "thinking" over their objectives. Then, when they face their first hurdle, they quit. Take a firm vow to your self. This is not the moment to think about making this happen or how you can be able to overcome all the obstacles. Instead, cultivate the seed of your dreams in you and vow to nurture that seed until you are able to reap the rewards of your hard work.

Be true to your commitment to yourself. Nobody can deter you if you refuse to let it happen. Take a vow to what you're looking for and stand in your conviction. Whatever it may be or how daunting it may appear, you must decide to do it! Why? Because you're looking for something for yourself, and you've made the choice to buy it.

2. Surmont your fear.

When you are advancing toward your goal the fear and doubt will show up sooner than you thought. To overcome the fear of failure, it's helpful to know how to remove your self from this anxiety. As an example instead of thinking something such as "I'm worried about what might occur," he learns to use the words: "There is a part of me that is scared and isn't willing to go on. However, in my heart there is an urge to continue moving ahead. "

Fear is merely an emotion you are experiencing. It is important to acknowledge your fear, not to see yourself in the same way and to keep breathing. Breathing is a way to keep your energy flowing and helps prevent fear from devouring your. Therefore, breath! Tell yourself that, even although you're feeling fearful it is still possible to be proactive. Then look the fear with a smile and tell him: "You are not my owner" You can then take the steps to obtain new strategies and tools that will further your goal.

4. Develop the trust muscle.

Even though pursuing your desire can cause you to feel anxious, afraid or doubts. This journey is exactly what you require to boost your confidence. It's not enough you are able to make the right decisions even when it is easy and easy; you have to take action when the circumstances make it challenging for you. When you're carrying a great deal of pressure on your shoulders it is necessary to work through doubts. Making major decisions in stressful situations can help you achieve real personal growth and helps you realize your own inner transformation.

Self-confidence is the key ingredient to success."

Emerson

It's the challenges of your life's journey that provide you with hundreds of chances to build your confidence muscles and allow you to develop it based on your own experiences. Every setback, obstacle or failure gives you the chance to be confident in yourself and not fall into fear and doubt.

Chapter 7: When Self-Confidence Gets Too Exaggerated

There are many ways that a more extreme form of confidence an individual has in regards to himself or herself could be manifested. It could be due to ignoring or refusing to accept certain circumstances and the potential for continual improvement and growth because one has come to the conclusion that be able to go on and accept these situations which may provide positive effects on their wellbeing in the future, if they decide to accept them as they've been seen as something that one could do with no problem at all. Furthermore, the same individuals might come to the same conclusion, resulting in the belief that the individual has a superiority status in their abilities that they are unable to give up any opportunity to develop their skills since they fear that doing so will harm the image they have of themselves.

These negative perceptions may even take a turn to the contrary, where one believes they have superhuman capabilities that allows them to manage several opportunities, some of which are not compatible with the abilities they have acquired and because of their inability to rebut these possibilities since they realize that they will never be able to accomplish all of them because they do not have the skills to manage these tasks effectively. The burden of obligations rises significantly as a result, but there is a chance that this inflated level of confidence one displays towards them can lead to friends and family members who form the basis of the intimate circle of friends to disengage themselves from the perception that they don't recognize the cocky mentality that an individual has displayed in recent times. The people in the business group that an individual might be involved in may have similar feelings if they notice that their colleague has begun to appear too confident in their abilities when, in fact they have certain abilities that they do not have. A lack of confidence in oneself regarding the abilities of others can cause a person to beginning to overlook the value and abilities that their intimate partner in their relationship is trying to improve and further develop when they begin to put all of their efforts on exaggerating the amount of time they devote to showing off the capabilities of their respective partners during the process.

The research that examined the potential negative impacts that could be linked to someone who has been identified to have a high feeling of confidence in their capabilities and confidence in themselves has led to findings that have revealed that children in particular who showed an extremely strong sense of confidence in their abilities to perform and have an positive and positive view of themselves were more likely to be engaging in activities where there was a possibility that they would find themselves in a position where their wellbeing was at risk. It was also found that those with a higher degree of confidence in their capabilities were significantly more confident to the level that was thought as excessive. They was found to be involved in romantic relationships that were toxic and unhealthy, as these types of people exhibit a behavior tendency to avoid situations in which their relationship an issue primarily to the person has a romance with. The people with these more extreme convictions about their abilities were also discovered to have a tendency associated with being more violent and physically intimidating to others.

Naturally, that's not to say that individuals do not have the ability to show confidence. In fact, as discussed in chapter three there are a lot of positive effects of self-confidence that can be seen in a person. Sometimes, individuals who have a level is a confidence level in capabilities that appears to be exaggerated can result in an individual having a higher likelihood of achieving an accomplishment or be used as a way to trick others to reach an assumption that they can actually fulfill certain obligations even though the actual skills they are able to master don't necessarily correspond with the work they claim to be able to really do. However, there is a disadvantage of having a high degree of confidence related to the traits displayed by an individual in their own personality. These traits can be linked to a problem of being narcissistic or even suggesting that one is deceitful and untrustworthy, all of which aren't admired by anyone, and especially people who work in the corporate world , and are looking for employees who can take on the jobs they offer at moment.

There are instances where self-confidence could rise in certain people at times such as, for instance, situations in which this happens could result in someone becoming unrealistic about meeting deadlines or not putting forth the highest effort that they is able to give when performing the task which has been given to them but then being a victim and the consequences which result from the choices made. This is because they have to confront the negative consequences of such choices in nature that allow people who are in such a situation to think about the options they wish to take in the near future and devise strategies they can put into use in order to leave positive perceptions of colleagues and the supervisors in their full-time or part-time company. This is particularly true in the event that they recently faced the cost for work that did not meet the highest standards of excellence that he or could cultivate. But, in these circumstances, it's not a terrible situation to fall into when people are able to take the lessons learned from the mistakes they've made and progress into better people and professionals. Naturally, the opposite path is in stark contrast to the types of people who discover that their behaviors have transformed into typical behaviour that are an even more challenging issue and show a degree of performance and attitude toward himself or herself which is not a good fit and could cause their lives to fall into a downward spiral in the process.

In this moment you may be wondering about how someone is able to transmit the beliefs they have with regards to their abilities into an altered appearance that makes their confidence in themselves to not be perceived as positively that it was before. There's no specific way in which these potential harmful changes could occur, based on the strategies that their parents utilized to define the type of person this individual will be once the time comes to reach the point maturation in his or her lives and the beliefs and values that form the basis of the culture the person was urged to live by and follow throughout their life. Additionally, the most significant events that resulted in such drastic or even minor shifts to take place within an individual as they begin to be more or less conscious of the person they are transforming into and their personal attitudes and perspectives begin to emerge. In our own perspective the things we want and what we need as well as what we've been through so far in our lives and the attitudes we display toward ourselves, and what kinds of cognitive processes be circulating through the broadest areas in our minds are thought to have a greater importance over what others think about themselves, the conditions and situations they face and what others need and the desires of others. There are additional studies that clarify the beliefs that people display toward themselves, in the sense that, due to the fact that some people believe that they are superior or they are able to complete certain tasks, this could cause them to overstate the things they are capable of doing. The way they see themselves as to them forming their own methods of looking at things that have nothing to be associated with them, and then transforming the subject to reflect only what they've gone through in their lives and the beliefs they express and also focusing exclusively only on their own views about the subject instead of allowing an opportunity to consider the thoughts of others. In the end, it's best to be aware of yourself that is reflective of the person you are, not the person you are trying to be in an effort to look more confident in general. In chapter 5 I will go into more detail on the various strategies people use to show their new-found confidence in the future.

Chapter 8: Practical Strategies To Increase Confidence

When you've got the foundation established to feel confident and confident, you are now able to do the things you can do to help you build it. Following the same routines you've used to do is only going to get you more of what you've always had! That's why it's essential to make changes that are practical to build your confidence. Here are a few steps you can follow:

Step 1: Record Yourself

Videotaping yourself allows you will be able to see what you look like to other people. It may seem strange initially, and most likely, you will not like it. Why? because we're always more hard on ourselves than we will ever be. However, by recording yourself, you'll be able to assess how confident you are. If you aren't happy you're able to work on the issue and then re-videotape.

Step 2. Get enough regular sleep

A restful night's sleep can't be undervalued. Don't watch television right before bedtime since your sleep won't be as relaxing. Additionally, you should go to sleep at a regular time each night and try to achieve this even on weekend. A majority of people require 7-8 hours of rest each night. There are four or five known cycles of sleep that you experience each night. The most memorable dreams will occur in the last cycle of sleep. Dreams assist you in processing information and data and permit you to know what the frequency of your vibration is. So, get good sleep.

Step 3: Develop new hygiene habits cleaning, brushing and flossing

If you're not establishing healthy habits for your hygiene routine, now is the best time to start. Making sure you floss every day for those who are prone to gingivitis is crucial but is one of the most easy things to avoid. This is where the willpower comes in! It is possible to make it your goal to floss only one tooth, and to keep it up every throughout the day! So that when you're cleaning that tooth, you'll likely floss the rest of your teeth as well!

Step 4: Add more effort in your hair and appear like a million dollars

Your hair speaks volumes about your character. It's among the physical characteristics of women and men that people pay attention to. Therefore, you must take good care of your hair the best as you can to ensure that it will reflect your confident, new self.

Step 5: Try something different in your appearance

Have you observed that many women change the color of their hair or alter their appearance after breaking up? This is actually a good option to take. Women may colour their hair cut it or do some other thing to alter their appearance. Whatever it is. Often it's a matter of changing things up following a breakup. Making changes to your appearance is an affirmation towards yourself and others to show of the fact that your life has changed. It's an extremely healthy way keep yourself in mind that things have changed and you're evolving.

Sixth Step: Get dressed more professionally and feel better.

"Success is not more than some simple rules, which are applied every day." Jim Rohn.

Most of us find that the more stylish you look the better you feel. Don't spend a fortune to achieve this however dressing as elegantly and within the budget you have is good. Why? Because it will make you feel better! Don't forget, you're not doing it for the sake of others You are doing it to yourself.

While it's always ideal to not be concerned about what people think of you The attitude you need to cultivate can be described as: "I want to look good , so I feel great, and not because I am concerned about what other people think of me." The most important thing is the way you feel about yourself.

Step 7: Exercise Regularly

Exercise is likely to be among the most crucial things you can do to improve your self-confidence.

Training and exercising helps to maintain your body's strength helps prevent disease, decreases stresslevels, improves the immune system. It aids you think more easily, and also helps to feel great about yourself.

Jack LaLanne used to be asked this question: which exercise is the most effective?

His response was to say that he was doing that he was training for weights. Why? because it helps strengthen the muscles of your body, oxygenates your the entire body, helps strengthen bones, and aids you appear and appear younger. It's the most effective anti-aging option you have.

If you are not a fan of lifting weights there are many fantastic exercises you can try. You can bicycle run, walk, ride or climb to play baseball, basketball football, or whatever sports you are interested in.

The most effective thing you can do to establish the healthy habit of exercise is to choose a sport that you like and do it with a friend. If you have someone who you can exercise with, it's more enjoyable to take part and do it. With a partner, it's more enjoyable, fun, and also makes it easier to conquer any resistance that you might experience.

How much exercise is actually necessary? According to studies conducted by Harvard the majority of us ought to be getting at least 2 1/2 hours of aerobic activity every week. An hour of exercising each day is typically enough to meet the guidelines for exercise. They conducted an investigation of 14,000 women, and followed them throughout 13 years. They wanted to determine what amount of exercise these women need to perform to keep their weight within the 5 pound limit.

The study revealed that the women had to train for at least an hour each day to keep their weight. This seems like an awful lot of effort to maintain the weight you are at, however it is contingent on your diet, too. Whatever you decide to do, you must maintain balance.

"Physical Activity Guidelines What Exercise is Your Body Needing?" The Source for Nutrition. Source. Harvard, 20 Nov. 2013. Web. 20 July , 2015.

Step 8: Practice using your voice more loudly

Your voice is an vital indicator of your confidence. It is well-known that a loud clear voice is an indication of confidence. A weak, soft-spoken voice isn't.

It's a great opportunity to look over yourself in your video. Are you confident and confident? What is your voice like? Are you talking clearly and loud enough?

Many of us who aren't typically confident in our abilities tend to talk in a soft manner. Practice speaking loud and clearly to anyone you meet for just one hour and observe the changes in how people react to your words. You may surprise yourself!

Chapter 9: Self-Confidence Self-Fulfilling Prophecies And Virtuous/Vicious Circles

In the final chapter, we started to understand the mechanisms of confidence that work or not working in relation to interactions and approaches. With this knowledge, it is possible to see the ways in which a normally confident mindset can be self-fulfilling prophecy, and is an enormous asset in the dynamics that are based on sexual desire. In the end the process of self-fulfilling prophecy may determine the course of a lifetime's relationship with women either in a positive or negative way.

Everybody knows someone who isn't very attractive beautiful, trendy, rich or any other thing who can pull off an impressive amount of women. The majority of the time such a person is just an average guy who believes in himself and wants women to love him simply because.

On the other hand everybody also knows someone who is said to under-perform with women because of the self-fulfilling of their low expectations. The same way I've seen a few successful "losers" who self-generate attraction through belief I've met a number of handsome, popular, and attractive men who have completely ruined their potential due to expecting to be constantly failing.

In any case, the combined beliefs produce the results through the contagious emotion mechanism that then lead to various forms of proof that extend the circle to the belief system and patterns of thought.

One who believes that he is in a relationship with women is a failure and is unsure of his ability to attract women will display fear via his appearance, voice tone, and general behavior with any woman is in contact with. Naturally, this is an important factor in his being dismissed, rejected or thrown out into the darkness of the "friend zone". He will later be able to reflect on these repeated negative situations and think of himself as in a way a failure. The circle is completed and the man will become more and less appealing.

I would like to see you not stuck in this vicious cycle. I was there for a short time in my younger years, and it's my responsibility to assist men in getting to break out of this vicious cycle and get back on the right path.

A man who believes that he is attractive and attractive to women, is 'cool' and generally successful in relationships with women will emit a relaxed and a masculine, confident appearance through his voice and body language when interacting with the majority of the women they meet. These traits of interpersonal relationships can be a major factor in creating sexual attraction from the beginning in many instances. If he thinks about these successes they provide further evidence to support his confidence in himself. The circle is completed. This is the way and method you must to aim for and be aware of as the road you're following regardless of the obstacles that will occur in the beginning of trying to alter your life and the way you feel.

I'm still remembering the day I determined to be better at engaging with girls One of my first girls I came across was a promising possibility. We had scheduled a time to meet , but she disowned me and did not ever contact me again. I was devastated angry, demoralised, and disappointed. It's possible to experience this feeling when you attempt to change something that you are experiencing, but the more crucial thing is to keep your goals in mind and never give up on the change you've set out to make for your self in the long run.

There are moments of setbacks and disappointments in all endeavours in life. The most important thing is to find the strength that surpasses these setbacks, to utilize failures as a learning experience and learn from them and to keep going to stay the course. The next section, I will detail the habits you must adopt and constantly remind you of them when the going is tough.

In the end, the more difficulties that you can reframe and overcome, and then make use of as learning tools for advance your career to become an incredibly confident and powerful beast you'll eventually become.

So, you must commit to a long-term path and make a change. Don't look at my books thinking that you'll become an example of confidence to the next woman you meet. If you do fall in love with it quickly, or even something else, it's an added benefit. In the long run any setbacks you are able to get off and build from will be of more importance. They will be the defining of you as you review every experience and travels in a wider perspective.

I've often noticed that it's those who are the most intelligent men who have the greatest issues in their confidence around women. They think too much about things. In contrast, a dumb person is getting more than they deserve because they're not thinking enough to think about anything other than the things that are under their eyes at any given time.

A more critical reader might have noticed some slight contradictions in my suggestions. It's possible that you're thinking it's not logical to consider every positive result as confirmation that you're stunningly attractive, while all rejections are nothing more than feedback and aren't based about how attractive to women you are. If you think that, you're right, then. It's not logical. Men who have confidence in women usually don't even think about it enough to bring it up in their minds that their personal beliefs don't really make sense when you look at it.

Let it go and accept it go. If you analyze something to a certain extent, you'll find some sort of paradox or conflict. When you encounter this kind of thing the result is more significant than the knowledge. Simply follow the flow. Keep things that'make sense to you for other aspects of your life. There are men (perhaps you) who drive themselves into a state of disorientation thinking that women do not make sense'. This is a subject which I try my best to deconstruct into sensible , practical principles However, when too much analysis can lead to confusion, may not be clear or worse, the actions that follow you need to develop the discipline of understanding it within your head before taking action to action.

A few men who enter this kind of situation may face difficulties in this field when they're at a high degree of success. Their appreciation for things that are being going well and the improved confidence that it provides is a double-edged saber. The more faith they place on anything that is positive about women, they will experience the unintended negative effect of rejections hitting them more. Don't be thinking that way. If women are in love with you and can't just wait to be into the bed with you, that means you're the one to beat. If she has no desire for you It's just a sign that the worst happens, and you'll appear more relaxed and attractive the next time around.

Take this approach and you'll be on your path to a positive cycle of self-confidence. At the end of the day it'll be more pleasurable to join the men who don't think or even analyze about what women want now and can simply move through the world of sexual sex and attraction effortlessly as opposed to join the group of "pickup artist" types who constantly think about everything and can never escape the changing levels of masculine self-confidence.

The ultimate destination or aim is not to consider any of these things in a way that is analytical. Analyzing the principles is an important step , but it's is merely a step. At the end of the day, the principles are only something you can come to for a refresher every now and then or when you are in a particularly stressful situation. The so-called "naturals" with women regardless of their intelligence level should not be concerned about how each and every aspect works or what is the best method to approach women and should not worry about it when learning is fully integrated.

The top of the virtuous circle confidence is an unconsciously competent. A model of learning suggests that four different stages that a person experiences are: conscious incompetence, conscious incompetence conscious competence, and finally unconscious competence. The last one is probably established in your head as your long-term target when it comes down to women and sexual sex especially in the area of confidence. You can also adopt an unprejudiced attitude towards undesirable outcomes.

Chapter 10: Understanding The Importance Of Discipline

I've got a sign up on my wall which simply reads:

Discipline = Power, Confidence and PROGRESS

What is self-discipline?

Discipline means the capacity to force yourself to act regardless of your mood.

Imagine what you could achieve If you were able to simply force yourself to stick to your ideals regardless of what. Imagine yourself telling yourself, "You're overweight. Reduce twenty pounds." If you're not disciplined enough, this goal won't be realized. However, with enough self-control and discipline, you'll be able to achieve it. The peak of self-control is when you get to the point where you make a choice, it's almost guaranteed that you'll stick to the decision.

Self-discipline is among the numerous personal development tools that you can use. However, it's not the only solution. But the issues self-discipline is able to solve are crucial and, although there are many other methods to tackle these issues but self-discipline completely slams these issues. The ability to discipline yourself can help you beat any addiction or shed any weight. It will eliminate any disorder, procrastination or insanity. When it comes to the problems it is able to solve, self-control is unbeatable. Furthermore, it can be an extremely effective teammate when paired with other tools such as motivation, goal-setting and planning.

Self-Discipline and Building Self-Discipline

My method of how to develop self-discipline can be explained through an analogy. Self-discipline can be compared to an muscle. The more you work it, the more powerful you will become. The less you practice it and the less it is, the weaker.

Like everyone else has a different strength in their muscles and physical strength, we all have various levels of self-discipline. Everyone has some when you are able to keep your breath for in a matter of seconds you're probably self-disciplined. However, not all have achieved their discipline to the same extent.

Like it takes muscles to build muscle and self-control to develop self-discipline.

The method to develop self-control is similar to the use of the progressive method of weight-training to construct muscles. That means you should lift weights that are near your limits. When you exercise you are lifting weights that you're able to lift. The muscles are pushed until they are exhausted, then you take a break.

The same way for building self-discipline is face challenges that you are able to be successful at but aren't at your limits. It's not about trying to do something and failing each day or keeping in your comfortable zone. There is no gain in strength lifting the weight you can't move or increase your strength when in lifting weights that are too heavy for you. Start with the weights or challenges that you are able to lift, but are close to your limits.

Progressive training is when, once you've succeeded, you will are able to increase the level of challenge. If you continue to train using the same weights and exercises, you will not get more powerful. If you don't manage to test yourself in the world it won't help you gain greater self-control.

Like the majority of people who have weak muscles in comparison with how powerful they might develop through training, the majority of people are extremely poor in their self-control.

Let's take a look at an illustration.

If you're looking to build the capacity to perform eight hours of hard work every day, because you are confident that it will have a significant impact to your career. While listening to an audio show this morning which cited research that found that the typical office worker will spend 37 percent of their time unproductive social activities as well as other distractions that consume more than half of their time by consuming non-productive activities. Therefore, there's plenty of room to improve.

Maybe you attempt to complete all day long without allowing yourself to be distracted, and you're able to only accomplish it one time. The next day, you don't succeed to the point of failure. This is fine. You completed one repetition over 8 hours. Two hours is too much for you. Therefore, cut it back a little. What time period would you need to complete 5 reps (i.e. an entire week)? Can you concentrate for one hour every day, for five days in consecutive days? If you're not able to accomplish this, reduce it by 30 mins or however else you can manage. If you're successful (or in the event that you feel it could be too easy) Then raise the level of difficulty (i.e. you will be able to overcome).

When you've achieved an entire week at a certain level and you're ready to take it up step the following week. Continue this gradual training until you've achieved the goal you set for yourself.

Discipline is doing things that are hard or unpleasant. It helps strengthen your self-control and character. It helps you to be more determined. In turn, it increases your confidence in yourself.

The importance of discipline is in regards to your well-being as well as taking proper care of your body and taking care of your finances, and everything else!

If you declare that you'll take on something that is difficult, but it is beneficial to you and then you do it repeatedly and often... you'll significantly boost your confidence in yourself.

I have a list of what I refer to as"my "POWER REGIMEN".

It's my normal routine for the day.

It's something like this:

- Rise at 06.00

- Stretch/Yoga

Create a connection with goals / visualize or Incantation and Prayer Thankfulness

- Plan your day / KNOW YOUR OUTCOME

- Exercise 30 minutes

30 minutes of reading/learning

- Take 15 minutes to meditate.

- - Sleep at 22.30

When you exercise discipline and self-control, you build your confidence in yourself.

Set a goal for yourself and stick to the promise for 10 consecutive days. Watch how you feel, and feel the amount of power it can give you.

Discipline is an act of love! Be a good example of self-love! You are very important, so behave this manner! Make sure you take care of your body.

Exercise IX

Write down your personal "Power Schedule" What are you committing to doing to yourself each day?

You must be honest

Integrity requires you to be straight with yourself.

Sometimes, it's the most difficult task you'll ever complete... however, it's also the base of a happy life, self-expression, strength... everything.

Don't say "yes" to please others or simply because it's the right choice or because it makes you "look nice".

Self-confidence is the foundation for confidence. being in line to your beliefs.

If you're sure that you're doing the right thing the world will fall around you, and you'll be able to keep tranquility, peace of heart, and confidence.

Integrity is a must for confidence in yourself. It is a crucial quality to possess, and it's more than just an attribute since it makes sure that your other values are cherished and exemplified in a way that is consistent with.

If you don't want to have a amount of integrity, you shouldn't be able to put it away when it's not practical.

When you've chosen your values, you'll never alter your values. This is the metric of your worth as human being. If deep inside you are sure that you will never breach your most sacred values and you're at peace and confident.

Honesty means not only being honest, but also acting in the truth. If we pretend to be in a mood or pretend to love things we do not like and then we lose our self-esteem. If we lie, then we send our self the impression that truth is something that we must be ashamed of.

If we are able to pretend or act in a false manner we're denying our authentic self and this can create an unflattering self-image that we'll observe in the actions of those around us.

In his seminar Gary King deliver's his talk on The Power of Truth (www.thepoweroftruth.com) during an Anthony Robbins "Unleash the Power Within" seminar.

He said that Truth Honesty, Integrity, and Truth are the most important pillars for a happy and fulfilling existence... but also also the most infrequently practiced.

Are you actually observing your LORD'S WORD in your daily life?

Exercise X

What would you change If integrity were your most important quality? In what areas in your life do you feel "out of your integrity"?

Determine to return to Integrity in all of those areas in the coming month.

Chapter 11: The Foundation

In this section, I will discuss the precise principles behind five fundamental movements, the basic ones! If you can master these fundamental moves, you'll be ready for any kind of exercise. The five fundamental movements listed above are the base for any exercise at the gym and that's the reason I've picked these five movements. "The FAB 5 "are: the deadlift, the squat as well as the lift-up bench, pull-up along with the overhead shoulder press. In the pages to come I will detail each exercise and go over the exercises from A to Z.

Before I go into the in-depth analysis of every one of these exercises I thought I'd present them individually and provide you with a brief background on why I picked these workouts as FAB 5 exercises for you to include in your workout routine. The squat is among the most effective exercises that to do when you're stressed out. It is a great exercise for your whole body, whether you are using extremely heavy weights or do it using only your body weight. But, all squats aren't the same and, for the sake of this article to discuss the squat, we'll define a squat by the point at which your ankles are slamming against your butt or as I prefer to call it, "ass to grass."

The other exercise is deadlift. As opposed to the squat exercise it is not a weight that is placed on your body, but on the floor. Your objective is to grab the weight without benting or the spine is rounded. If you can imagine it, imagine a dog going into the toilet. In our case it's not important if you use a sumo or conventional pull and sumo; both will be discussed in the future. The only thing it matters is that you lift the weight off of the floor by using your legs.

The third and final exercise can be referred to as the bench press. This is a cousin to the push-up. It is the only thing anyone will ask you when they find out you are working out: "So, how much do you bench?"

Fourth exercise: the pull-up. This is a classic exercise that is associated with strength as I am prone to thinking in extremes. You can imagine yourself facing the tragic event of an accident that left you hanging off an rock. Do you think you could climb yourself back to safety? This is why the pull-up.

The last, but certainly not least is the overhead press. The overhead press is considered to be one of the most difficult exercises you'll ever complete at the fitness center. You are actually in a disadvantage mechanically when you attempt to push any kind of weight on your head using your small and flexible shoulders. Being able to do this task without bending either your spine or your legs an obstacle in and of itself. I've struggled for years with overhead presses with regards to massive hypertrophy or weight lifting. My personal highest weight, prior to the majority injury to my shoulders was at 205lbs. I could have weighed around 170 pounds.

After I've introduced these exercises in detail, we can begin how to complete each.

THE SQUAT

If you do it correctly, this workout will test your physical, mental and neurologic capabilities. It doesn't matter if it is a lifting device or you're performing the exercise against gravity only employing the weight of your body. Squats are essential to our lives. If we're getting out and in our vehicle or getting up from our chairs at work, we're performing the Squat. It is important to get proficient in it to avoid problems at work. This is a triple extension exercise for the lower body, namely exaggeration of the hips and knees, and ankles. The hip extension occurs when the hip is closed and gradually opens. When you perform this exercise the knee is the closest to the chest because of an angle that is lower of the hip's crease. The knee extension is an exercise that straightens your legs. The angle of your knee is rising. Ankle extension within the sagittal plan (plane of motion that creates a left and right split in the side) is not as simple. Ankle extension in the sagittal plane is both dorsi flexion as well as plantar flexion. In the eccentric (upward) part of squatting, you're moving away from the floor and making the joint more angular. This is also known as plantar flexion. Imagine stepping onto the gas pedal in your vehicle and pushing away from the accelerator--that is the plantar flexion.

Image of triple extension

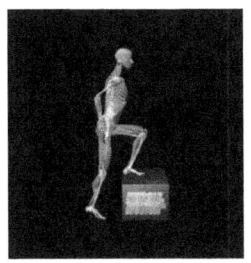

Do you feel like you can feel the squat woven throughout your day? Great! Another reason I've cited it as the primary reason as it's a vital an integral part of every day life. The perfect squat can be difficult to imagine if you've never done any exercise before or have shied away from them due to being scared of putting your spine on the line. I get it. With no weight, if you are able to sit your back on your ankles, as an infant, that's an ideal squat.

As we get older and are tethered to the desk and lose our natural childhood instinct to sit down and squat the way we would like. It's like sitting from the Squat. I'm here to assure that it is possible, not just to get it back and keep it.

Doing the Squat

In order to perform the squat you must have an appropriate amount of mobility in the hips as well as ankles. If you're too restricted in either of these joints, then performing the squat that mimics a toddler will need to wait until you've made your body more comfortable. Do some ankle mobility exercises and hip opening exercises or activities that ease stiffness that you experience throughout the day. In this article, let's assume you can perform the bodyweight squat in a way that your hips are lower than your knees, and your trunk is in a straight line and you are able to comfortably sit with your heels not raised.

The old adage, "don't let your knees get in the way of you toes" is to not raise your heel,. If you have trouble with this, you can try and practice it each day for about 10 seconds during your day. You could even lean your body against a wall and gradually distancing yourself from the wall at the same time looking straight ahead. Once you're comfortable in this position, you are able to begin adding weight. I suggest a goblet-style dumbbell for your first time and then hold the dumbbell beneath your cheeks (dumbbell head horizontal).

The goblet holds are an alternative that the front squat, due to the similarity in positioning and helps you are standing straight. When you are able to perform an squat goblet that is more than 45 pounds and you're at the point of trying the bar. A typical male Olympic bar at the gym weighs 20kg or 45 pounds. Likewise, the standard female Olympic bar weighs 15 kilograms (or 35 pounds). The bar should be placed in one of two locations that are directly over the traps (thick muscles that are located behind your head, which look like shoulder pads used by soccer players) or on your shoulder blades, or in mid-trap for a squat with a bar that is low (powerlifting method). The choice is yours, no matter what one you prefer with regard to bar placement , as both have the same components. The major distinction in bar placement is the central mass and your bar's path that you choose to use. If you put the bar over the shoulders of your body, then your body should be more upright. when you place it on your mid-trap, your body will tilt forward which forces you to alter the bar's path because it is more close than your hip. The high bar technique causes the bar closer to the knee , which lets you lower your hips further. Whatever the case, the signals for the rest body are similar.

For a properly executed back squat correctly, the bar should be placed on your shoulders and over your head. You'll need to prepare the rack to match the shoulder's height and for safety. For this, place up the "J-hooks" or resting spot for the bar, at the proper shoulder height, so you are able to move the bar into to and out, without hitting the rack (called "catching hooks").

The best method to make sure you are safe is to start with an incline stance that allows you to lift the the rack on your shoulders. I like to do squats this way due to the the ease of movement as I only need to move my foot. The staggered stance permits the user to increase weight and down without making contact with your J-hook. Because they're always placed below your shoulders, it means you don't need to be concerned about striking the rack in the beginning or the end of the workout. Safety first , and your ego last.

Once you've removed the bar (weight) Set your feet in a straight line, approximately hip width apart. If your heels are wider than your hips while toes are a bit further and out.

Brace yourself. Relax your breathing until you're prepared to begin your descent. When you're ready to begin, take the last breath and push the air up against the walls of your abdomen, and then back. Make use of your diaphragm for pushing the air to stimulate your trunk from your belly button to your spine. This is referred to in the medical world as "the brace." It is required to complete all five exercises.

Begin to descend as far as you are able in the final goal of getting your hamstrings or butts towards the back of your calf. This position is referred to as the lower position. When you are in the bottom position you can return to the top position by contracting to the maximum extent your quadriceps and gluteus maximus muscles and pushing your knees to the side. After you've "caught the bounce" you'll be back to standing. Repeat this process for the number of sets and reps you must complete during the day.

To rack the weight again move it forward and backwards into J-hooks. Don't get up on your toes and put it back. It will make it easier to lift in the event that you're trying to achieve the maximum effort and difficult attempts for example, a 1 repetition maximum (1RM).

Be sure to be sure to push your knees out. When your knees begin to collapse, the squat is an obvious sign of some limitation in your body.

The muscle may not be fully engaged or you're overly tight. Before you perform any load squats, it is recommended to take care to address any weaknesses with appropriate warming-up exercises for your body, known as movement preparations. The movement prep exercises address weaknesses within your chain of kinetics by providing the targeted effort. For instance, to strengthen the gluteus maximus muscle, which is weaker, you can do various exercises using the Mini-Band that you wrap around your knees. This could be something like glute bridges or clamshells.

The various issues mentioned above--ankle flexibility, hip mobility or knee collapse are indicators of an improper technique. To truly master the squat, it is essential that you have to address these problems. If you are experiencing problems with ankle flexibility, fix these issues early and regularly reinforce the flexibility during warm-ups. Do similar things with hip tightness or knee collapse. These are patterns of movement that you have learned in your daily or bad technique caused by years of incorrect technique. I would suggest that you correct any issues prior to trying to lift weights that are heavier. The reason for this is to allow your body to adapt slowly to a gradual method of overload. In simple way, what you're trying to achieve is adding the body with stress a tiny amount at a. The true mastery of your body won't happen over night and requires time. But so long as you can tackle any imbalance, injury or limitation, and get rid of your ego, you'll improve. The goal is to get every part of your body to be stimulated and flowing easily. Doing a squat where your ankles are in contact with your butt is not easy, but it is essential for your joint health in the long run, and that's why I'm trying to put my focus on: long-term health for joints as well as overall general health, so you can enjoy life.

Correct Squat Technique Using Bar:

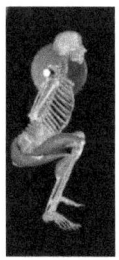

As I've mentioned previously it is commonplace to sit or stand all day long. The transition from standing to sitting is a squat, and there is an excuse not to do one. The reason why squats are extremely effective in training, aside from the physical demands it places on your body is because it's an ideal metaphor for living. The world is constantly demanding more of you. It is putting an ever-growing amount of burden onto your shoulders, and ultimately, it is burdening you. From your home life to work managing it all You are being pushed downwards and downwards, and the burden is extremely heavy. The only option is to fight back. Do you have the courage to do that?

Chapter 12: Habits You Must Follow Daily To Build And Increase Your Self-Esteem

Once you've figured out the ways to recognize and conquer the beliefs that limit you You can now begin to restore your confidence in yourself by increasing your self-confidence. In order to do this, first you need to alter your perception of yourself.

It is time to alter the way you think about yourself and your perception of yourself. Everyone has a self-perception. Everyone has a picture in their heads about who they really are, the things they're capable of and where they're headed.

If you are struggling with low self-esteem, you've got an unflattering view of these issues. You may feel like you're not worthy of anything, and that everything you do will end up in failing or mediocrity.

It is essential to improve your self-image if you wish to improve confidence in yourself and increase confidence in yourself. In order to begin the process of improving your self-esteem you should integrate these habits in your daily life.

Let yourself be forgiven

If there's any way to self-esteem that is healthy then this is it. If you can let go of your self-pity, you can take your self-esteem to a new level. It's about being kind to us and showing compassion not just for other people but also for us. (Do not think of this as self-pity, which is harmful.)

The reason we feel low self-esteem is the feeling of guilt for doing something or not completed, and so it's essential to let yourself forgive yourself. Once you've done this, you'll feel more confident about yourself and you'll be able to forgive others.

Give yourself a sense of forgiveness take responsibility for your mistakes and pledge to never repeat them. Also, accept the responsibility for your mistakes (you're just human and don't have to be flawless) and build to build your own strengths. Be forgiving of your mistakes and don't repeat them, if at all possible.

The changes you'll notice as you discover how you can forgive yourself is incredible! Sometimes, the disorder will disappear. often self-forgiveness can remove the previous blockage in energy and allows wealth to flow into your life. Do it now and observe how forgiveness will bring to you during your life.

Learn More

Another way to increase your confidence is to ensure that you acquire knowledge in your professional and personal activities. There's always that one aspect in which you feel that you lack knowledge and understanding.

If you're looking to build greater confidence, you must demonstrate your proficiency in this field. You can increase your knowledge through online classes or taking part in similar conferences and events and studying books. Another thing you can take advantage of while you gain knowledge is teleclasses , where you can participate in discussions and exchange ideas with other students. This can help to increase your confidence.

Change Your Self-Talk

Self-talk is simply the act of speaking to yourself, whether mentally or in public. It's any idea that comes to mind in response to external stimuli. The way you perceive situations will depend on the thoughts you tell yourself.

If you look at the negative, it can cause negative emotions, such as anger or anxiety. Positively thinking about the issue will result in positive feelings like happiness or excitement.

When you work to boost your self-esteem, you will become conscious of the self-talk that can lead to negative feelings. You can change it by using positive self-talk that promotes higher levels of self-esteem.

If, for instance, you're constantly affirming that you're overweight every time you glance at the mirror, you must take a break and replace your thoughts with positive words.

In this instance it is because you've learned to focus on the areas of your body which cause you to feel insecure, and then reinforce your anxiety through the words "I'm overweight."

If you can teach yourself to look at yourself in the mirror and admire your body, or concentrate on an area you feel confident about, eventually this will alter your self-image as well as your confidence.

Practice Affirmations

Affirmations are simple positive affirmations that you make about yourself to help change your negative thought patterns. You can use a series of affirmations each day you can use them in order to substitute self-talk that is negative.

Self-esteem can be improved through affirmations through the implantation of new beliefs that replace those beliefs that contribute to low self-esteem.

If you're trying to alter your automatic self-talk and negative thoughts It is beneficial to create a list of affirmations that you can replace the negative, old thoughts patterns you've established. When you practice them enough, the affirmations will begin to be embedded within your unconscious mind.

In the near future, we will go into more detail about affirmations that are positive in order to help your development of a strong confidence in yourself.

Stop Comparisons

It is important to realize that your uniqueness. It is also important to recognize that you don't know the whole picture and everybody puts on a facade to cover up their fears.

If you are comparing yourself to others, you're trying to compare yourself to the image others display in front of the entire world.

Everyone is plagued by thoughts, doubts judgements, fears, and other battles are fought in their heads.

It is also important to not make comparisons in order to feel better about yourself. It's tempting to do this in order to feed your self-confidence, but it quickly turns into an unending cycle.

If you are using comparisons to feel better the brain will employ them to create a feeling less. The only way to avoid this is to shut yourself from making comparisons between you and other people.

Eliminate the Judgment

Judgment is among the worst and effective habits you can create. However, very few of us are able to live their lives free from judgemental thoughts. True confidence and judgment are not compatible. It is impossible to feel genuine peace if they hold onto their opinions.

The habit of judging becomes part of our lives We do it naturally without realizing it. We see ourselves as a kind of punishment for not being perfect and we criticize others to make us feel better.

People who are content with themselves don't feel the need to judge others or even themselves.

The first step to freedom is to accept that there isn't anything perfect in the world.

It is important to accept yourself for who you are and treat everyone else in the same manner. Every person came into the world with different characteristics and have experienced different experiences that have changed us. We all have challenges to overcome. It is not fair to judge anyone.

Let go of guilt

Guilt is among the worst emotions as the entire world full with people who are afflicted by guilt. The most damaging part is that guilt is a useless emotion. A whole book could be written about the futility of this emotion. It would not be a problem when we felt guilty for a moment and then move on with our lives. Unfortunately most people are living with a constant sense of guilt.

Why do we feel guilty? We've been taught to feel guilty all of our life. Inconstantly or not in our early years the people we love and friends, as well as society schools, and religions have encouraged our guilt and reinforced it through rewards and punishment system.

As children, we were constantly reminded by everyone around us on a regular basis of our poor behavior , and they compared us with other children who were acting more well. Guilt was used as a way to keep us in check.

The downside is that this type of treatment makes us be a victim, even though we didn't commit anything wrong. Additionally, for an extended period of time guilt was a result of caring. If you really care , you have to feel guilty but if you don't take care of yourself and don't feel guilty, then you're a horrible person. There is nothing more absurd than that.

The guilt you feel does not help you in any way; it can cause you emotional harm and causes you to feel shameful. Be rid of guilt today. There's a huge distinction between guilt and taking the lessons you learned from your mistakes. Guilt is always punished and comes in a variety of kinds, such as anxiety, feeling of inadequacy confidence, self-esteem issues as well as a lack of self-esteem. the inability of valuing others and ourselves.

The best part is the greater you work to improve your self-esteem and your authenticity and being with the right people , the less guilt you'll feel. When you are feeling guilt, remember that it's not a good thing and take a lesson from the mistake. This is all you have to do.

Make sure you are focusing on your strengths

If you are often in the company of individuals who are toxic, they could be enticed to point out your shortcomings. Do not listen to them. While it's important to know about our weaknesses - and recognize them, but we don't need someone to constantly remind us that it's best to be aware and concentrate on our strengths.

What are your most important personal qualities and professional strengths?

What is it that you excel at over others?

What are your most significant personal and professional accomplishments?

What makes you special and powerful?

It's time to strengthen the muscles. Do them regularly and focus on them, the ones you've had and those you'd like to have.

Learn to Say NO

There are people in your life who attempt to convince you to perform certain actions even if you're not wanting to Sometimes, because we want to please everyone and please everyone else, we will respond "YES" in their direction, even the inner voice of our mind says "NO." If we accept a yes offer when we'd prefer not to "NO" can damage our self-esteem , and afterwards it's over, we may feel unhappy or even angry.

Learn to say "no" will improve your life significantly. You'll get more of you because every time you answer YES, even by saying NO, you lose the little bit of yourself and your self-esteem will decrease.

If you can decide that you believe that a "Yes" is an "Yes" and "No" is a "No" is an "No" and you'll feel more comfortable. This will mean less commitments and, while telling your family and friends "NO" is difficult initially however, the results are extremely positive.

People who are most effective will say "No" often. Therefore, make sure to use the word "NO" without feeling guilty.

Be Positive and Surround Yourself with Positivity

It's not a wise choice to blame our failures on anyone else, sometimes others can be the ones the cause of our low self-esteem. This is particularly true when we are a part of people who aren't our ideals - or when our friends tend to point out our weaknesses instead of encouraging us and praising our accomplishments.

That's why it is important to stay away from the people who are toxic. In fact, when you look at all that we've said in the previous chapter, it's usually the ones who are not confident who are driven to test their abilities and harm our lives. We are made to feel inadequate in order to make them feel larger.

If you have a list of people who are toxic and negative such as this, then try to avoid hanging out with the same kind of people. Also, you must spend more time with positive people you love.

If you have to be around those who have a negative impact on your self-esteem? Consider the motives behind everything they make public. If they're expressing criticism of you, are they really believe that you've committed a mistake? Or , is it because they're insecure? Perhaps they're just someone who is negative? Do not let that affect the way you view yourself.

Make Improvements to Yourself

We all have issues about us. However, most of the time, those aspects can be changed. In fact, the mere attempt to improve is often enough to increase our confidence in self-esteem.

If you are unhappy with the way you look, you should think about how you can enhance your appearance to appear more attractive. If you feel too slim or 'tiny', you can bulk up. If you are feeling overweight, you should reduce weight. If you feel you're a bit slow-witted, improve your conversational skills. If your math lets you down, go get lessons!

Integrate Self-Care

Self-care neglect could lead to a low self-esteem and is an indicator of self-esteem issues. Self-care is simply doing something to make you feel happy.

It could be as easy as taking a relaxing bubble bath, taking massage, or even taking the time to walk with yourself. Self-care is usually viewed as selfishness. Many people feel guilty about taking time for themselves since they feel it's taking away the joy of others.

The first step in changing this is to realize that you deserve attention and time, and let go of any thoughts that trigger guilt. The next step is to identify one thing you could incorporate every day that is 100 % for you.

Inform your family and friends that you're doing this and remain as dedicated your self as you were to everyone else.

Get rid of Perfectionism

The concept of perfectionism is often used as a cover-up to hide anxiety. It's also the biggest adversary of confidence. The root of perfectionists is the belief that you have to be perfect in order to earn respect and love from you and other people.

It means that the person puts their self-worth on the basis of accomplishments and defines the self-concept of a person through actions. This type of thinking can cause drastic shifts in confidence and moods, as well as the pressure to always do the right result.

You must get rid of your perfectionist tendency. You need to cultivate unconditional love and respect of yourself. You must realize that you are independent of your actions and your accomplishments.

The more likely you are to be accepting of yourself even when you fail the better your self-esteem will increase.

Celebrate Daily Victories

It can be daunting when we attempt to alter the way we live our lives. Changes can take time and they will only be possible through regular actions.

There are plenty of individuals who were capable of overcoming anxiety and gain confidence in themselves however, it didn't happen over night. To keep yourself on the way to improving confidence in yourself and building confidence, you must acknowledge and celebrate small successes.

Small victories that you celebrate while working towards a target will help increase confidence. You are worthy of recognition and need to be prepared to grant yourself acknowledgement. If you're constantly focusing on how far off you are from achieving the end of your journey the journey might become a battle full of doubt and despair.

Instead, you should celebrate the small achievements along the way and you will feel filled with positive energy and motivation to keep going.

Be thankful for the things you Are Having

People who are self-defeating tend to dwell on bad experiences and shortcomings in their lives. It's easy to dwell on the things you would like but you don't have and it is a lot of work to alter your outlook.

Giving thanks and appreciation for every aspect of your life will change your outlook at every moment, and ultimately alter your perspective of the world and yourself.

When you practice gratitude, take time to be grateful for the abundance of blessings in your life and for the person you are as an individual. Make a list of three distinct things you are grateful for in yourself, and three things you are thankful to have in your daily life. You can incorporate a routine of gratitude to yourself and others every day and observe the impact it makes on your self-esteem overall.

Engage in a Passionate Faith

One of the traits I like about confident people is that they believe in a higher power. They believe that God, the creator of all things has a plan for every living soul. Also the reason we exist on earth in this moment is to accomplish our purpose in life.

In the same way, they appear to be in complete control and when they stick to the blueprint of their creator, success is only a matter time. If you really desire to be successful then you need to believe that it's feasible. It is crucial to believe in your capabilities. If you believe with passion, you are more likely that you will fulfill the path you've chosen to follow.

Create realistic expectations

The fastest way to destroy you confidence is setting lofty standards for yourself. Making goals as well as working towards these goals can boost confidence. But, if you set yourself up for failure You will be left feeling disappointed.

If you have a goal you would like to work towards set an achievable goal that you can start working on right now. Set goals that are small and manageable, and remember to celebrate every small win.

You can be confident

Did you realize that expectations are faith in your actions? In this moment, you have already imagined yourself being confident and how that will affect you. If you're confident, you speak, move, and act effortlessly and with such determination as you strive to achieve your goals. It is the moment you realize that you are able to see and emotions as well as the actions of a confident individual. That is, you'll be in a better position to go above and beyond your expectations. If you believe you can be confident that confidence becomes an actuality.

As we've already mentioned that confidence isn't something that is created in a single day. You must continue to apply these practical tips to practice over the course of months. Start by writing down the ways you plan to implement the action plans. This way, you will know exactly what it would be to move toward your goals. If you take action on these you begin to notice dramatic gains in your confidence which in turn leads into solid faith, happiness, joy and finally, happiness in your life.

Chapter 13: Strategies For On The Day Of The Event

Conducting research and applying those positive-visualization techniques mentioned in previous chapters can assist in getting ready for your event in the days prior to the event. These techniques can help you increase your confidence about the things you need to accomplish and enable you to be equipped with the necessary knowledge and skills to be successful in the event of your presentation, meeting or even date. Even if you're organized, the following guidelines will help you go one step further and give you an advantage when it comes to the event the event itself.

#1: Get Sleep Well

It's pretty obvious However, in the evening prior to your important appointment be sure to have enough sleep. Adults require between 7 to 8 hours of rest each night to be at their best. You are aware of what your body demands, so make adjustments to the amount that you require to stay rejuvenated. The day before the interview, follow your positive-motivation routine early in the morning. It is also possible to exercise , if you normally do, in order to keep in good spirits and alert. Also, make sure you eat a nutritious breakfast that is brain-healthy in before the occasion. Include Omega-3s for good brain function, to remain alert and focused. Also, eat low glycemic index whole grains that provide a gradual and steady discharge of power throughout your day.

For a spy each day is an important day. This is why I recommend having a healthy routine you adhere to. It helps you start every day in a positive way, and it also provides the consistency to build your confidence because you're prepared to start every day in a healthy way.

#2: Take Time for Yourself

Are you the kind of person who has missed something due to a delay that you felt like your heart was race and you wondered if you'd arrive on time, or if you'd be able to be late for your appointment or be punished by your boss or face another set of consequences? Being late is not an advantage, as it indicates poor planning. It is also possible to make mistakes such as not putting on deodorant or not brushing your hair when you rush to get dressed. This is not a nice style.

Begin by laying out your clothing the night before, and making sure that everything is simple to locate the next morning. Also , keep your keys to your car, wallet as well as any other materials will be required for the occasion to ensure that you don't forget any essentials. Get up early and give you plenty of time to plan your day. Leave your home within 30 minutes to avoid having to rush. It is not a good idea to arrive exhausted or, more sweaty since you needed to get to it in time.

#3: Create a Fantastic First Impression

When the first time someone sees you, their minds will begin to evaluate your appearance and make judgements. This is why it's crucial to dress appropriately and smell nice, as well as keep yourself well-groomed when you attend an important appointment, date or even a meeting. Apart from all these factors, you must to make the necessary steps to establish a strong connection and convey an impression of confidence telling everyone that you're sure of your own. When greeting everyone you meet, make sure to address them by name. Also, make sure you are using a firm, solid handshake and eye contact with others. These are the basic skills that people who are confident use, and they will prove that you're a strong person who is confident of yourself. This will put everyone at relaxed.

#4: Be Present in the Present (Situational Awareness)

It is impossible to give a great presentation or have a memorable date if you're continuously wondering how the event is going to end , or what the other person is thinking. If you are engaged in something, it's essential that you give it all your attention. Try to be in the present moment, taking note of your surroundings and paying focus on the expressions of the other person and also your own.

While you're supposed to be in the present however, it's recommended to consider at least a few steps ahead. Preparing yourself for the questions that might come up or having small conversations can help you prepare for this and you should pay attention to what's happening so that you can alter your approach in case of need. Looking a few seconds in the future if you anticipate responses or questions is a smart strategy when it does not remove you from the present. However, you shouldn't look to far ahead that you're worrying about what's going to happen rather than focusing your attention on the work that is in front of you.

As an agent of the law, you need to be able to live in the present moment and anticipate. It is crucial to recognize important signals and to respond to the situation is not a secret. This involves a lot with observing the people in your vicinity and paying to their body expressions and how they react to what you say. You can't absorb all the information when you're not fully engaged.

5. Learn about the Art of Small Talk

Small talk is a remarkably beneficial habit. Simply, speak to anyone! If you're going to an event, meeting or any other significant event Begin by speaking to people who are 'peripheral' within and around the venue. This is especially helpful when you're naturally than a little shy. The people you could discuss with include security personnel, door staff as well as waiters and anyone else you come across prior to the occasion.

The advantages of doing this is twofold. First, it relaxes you and helps you get prepared to talk. This is particularly beneficial for those who suffer from anxiety about approaching as it helps you get into a rhythm of communicating with others. Another advantage of small-talk is that you could be able to pick up a key piece of information you would not have otherwise. It could be something minor which can allow you to interact directly with someone or an the organization that you're scheduled to meet with. If a secretary informs you that the person you're waiting for has arrived late because he had to drop his son in soccer school, sneak into a conversation with him about the joy you feel watching your kids play soccer! There's no need to be a soccer player yourself...

This can be extremely useful when you're a spy, specifically the part about spotting interesting bits of details. When you're gathering intelligence about a person or an organization and want to talk to people who might know about their existence was a must. I can recall a time when I tried to talk with the CEO of a major company I was collecting information on. He was not willing to meet with me. When I tried to talk to him his secretary, she said it was already over. I tried to contact different people in the building, including the person who was in charge of the garage for parking. He was a bit puzzled when he pointed at the CEO's parking space which was full of his vehicle. I waited for him to leave before I finally began my research.

#6 6: Do a practice story Telling

The ability to craft a compelling story is useful in a variety of scenarios. It can be used to make a point about your presentation or break the ice during the business meeting or date or to answer a question during an interview. I've encountered many instances in my professional and private life when this technique can be useful. It was usually utilized as a way to avoid being caught if my protection was going to be threatened. When things were not going well and you were in a bad spot, a few canned stories could give you the space to move out of situations or give the extraction team to intervene if things were to get a bit tense.

Being able to become a great storyteller is also an extremely attractive and interesting personal trait. It helps ease tension in a variety of situations. Try to get comfortable telling stories that you can use in any situation you could encounter. This can help you in the event that you have to employ the following strategy.

#7: Always have an exit strategy

Sometimes, it's just necessary to leave the circumstance. If you have to get out of an unpleasant date or get from a presentation to take a moment to compose yourself, always find an exit plan, and still maintain a good manner of conduct. You can excuse yourself by pointing to an ice-cold drink or wait with a friend to receive the SOS text. You can think of ways that you aren't rude in the event that you're required to.

I once worked on an investigation into the Russian mafia in Budapest, Hungary, with some really tough guys who aren't one to offend. Because of the significant risk involved in that case the necessary precautions were implemented. I was wearing a tiny microphone that was tucked away inside the part of my pocket. We were much more discreet than you'll get in the movies thanks to all the wires secured to chests of people to monitor. Even with my calm , composed manner and a solid story behind it I could tell that the tape was beginning to look suspicious. Although he was speaking to me I could tell by his calm and tense posture as well as the little movement of his arms below his desk, that he might be planning to perform something. (One one of the activities that you'll always find yourself doing while spying is to watch people's hands. Hands that hold guns, knives or use punches. If they are hidden and is caught, they're usually in danger). He was probably planning to press an alert button which would signal his team to either remove me or draw an assault weapon on me. I was unsure whether I caused him some offense or if he was simply in awe of my deceit. Whatever the reason, I knew I was being investigated.

I was brought in to attempt to offer him a gun that was not registered. We wanted to find something to catch the suspect and hopefully nab the suspect to provide us with information regarding another case in which that we were working on. I was hired to track down the location of a prominent politician's daughter. It was unclear whether she was kidnapped by this group eager to extort her family or had gone missing, and they might be able to provide some clues that would aid in finding her.

I had a plan of escape before I even entered the scenario. My guys were taking off the roof and were ready to swiftly enter the ducts should they show any indication of trouble. I was aiming to find the closest exit. I had a look at the blueprints of the building prior to my visit to locate doors that could be used as well as windows. Before we took these options, I attempted to leave in a respectful manner. "Alright I can tell you're not interested. I'll be there in a minute," I gestured toward the door. "Hang for a second," he said stiffly in the Moscow language (I can speak Russian pretty well at this stage). When he denied my request to leave and walked away, I knew that things were going to turn horribly.

It turned out that I was correct on the button. Two massive, muscular men walked through the doors in the area. I quickly walked through the window. It might have been challenging to be located on the third floor however, there was a fire escape just outside waiting as I had guessed it was going to be. I quickly began to make my way to the escape. As I expected, the two men tried to track me. They began to shoot bullets, but most of them did not even come close to me. I heard "bang" and "bang" and one of them was screaming in pain. My team up there was doing their job making sure that I came out alive.

My exit did not be as stylish as I wanted it to be, I did get out of the way breathing. That's the most important thing to me. It's unlikely that you are a spy , however, so you need to strive for a bit better grace when you design how you will exit.

Most of the time in everyday life, it's all about having an excuse to make use of. A crucial meeting is something you have to attend in case the situation is not going well. Be sure to prepare for it in advance.

Hope that the strategies and concepts in this section of the book will have given you a solid foundation of the things you need to do to build confidence and trust in the preparation prior to an important event, as well as during the event which will allow you to perform optimally and gain the maximum benefit and enjoyment from the event.

The third and final part (part 3) will be the frosting to the cake. This is the time when you're in the middle. If you've implemented the advice from the previous chapter to use, you'll be on the right track. However, you'll need to be taught how to manage those moments that come upon you. The moments even the best-planned plans cannot anticipate. They frequently trigger sudden and abrasive episodes in social anxiety. This can be very debilitating for someone who doesn't know how to handle it properly. This won't be the case soon enough.

Chapter 14: Acknowledge Your Fears And Successes

Being aware of your child's fears and their achievements is essential in aiding your child develop confidence in themselves. This is particularly true when a child is able to overcome the fear that he or she has to accomplish the goal. It's important to remember this when you're trying to boost confidence in your child's self, every tiny success must be celebrated. Your child will greatly benefit by being able to acknowledge their achievement no matter how insignificant the task.

The next chapter will give you helpful information that will assist you in recognizing your child's accomplishments as well as worries. This chapter will act as your source of information, and you should pay to your surroundings and ensure that you take note of all the information because it will surely aid your child in becoming an confident person.

Recognize their achievements and sympathize with their anxieties

This chapter will discuss two issues: a parent's obligation to praise their child's achievements and acknowledging the child's fears. In order to build trust in your child it is essential for parents to recognize that both of them are equally important.

In the beginning, we'll talk about the importance of praising children's achievements and the best way to do it.

Recognize Their Achievements:

Recognizing your child's accomplishments however small they appear for you. It is crucial in helping to develop confidence. It will help your child feel proud of themselves and boost self-confidence as they will feel as if they are always making you feel special.

The act of praising your child's achievements instead of constantly criticizing the actions your child might engage in will have a much positive effect. This is because making a point of a child's errors can make them feel like they aren't capable of doing anything correctly. However you should always praise your child's achievements and not talking at them in regards to their shortcomings could have negative effects. The reason is that the child will be convinced that they are invincible and nothing could do wrong. It's crucial to strike a good balance between calling out mistakes and recognizing achievements.

If you are celebrating your child's achievements Be careful not to overindulge or spoil the child. If you offer your child an extravagant reward each after they have completed a minor exercise, they'll believe that this happens each time they finish something. If the rewards cease and the child is confused as to what they are not getting an award for completing a particular job, which can cause undesirable behavior. It is suggested that awards are reserved for greater achievement. For small accomplishments, a simple compliment or a simple compliment could suffice.

Know the fears of your child:

Knowing your child's needs is equally crucial to their development of confidence in themselves. You may be thinking about what can fear do to aid my child in becoming more confident in himself. The answer is that conquering anxiety can dramatically boost confidence in one's self. It is crucial to understand your worries before attempting to conquer them.

Don't place your kid in a place in which he or she could be unable to succeed. The things they're afraid to try are difficult for them to deal with. Placing a child in a scenario that they aren't able to be able to win is among the most unwise things you can be doing to build their confidence. It is important to talk with your child and find out what they're scared of doing, and decide if it's an appropriate idea to push your child to confront their fears.

When you have a clear comprehension of the concerns of your child and the possible negative and positive outcomes of engaging them, you'll be able to determine whether you want to invite children to speak up. One of the most effective ways to increase confidence in children is to take on an endeavor which they had previously believed they'd fail at. This is due to the fact that this process shows youngsters that if they put their minds on accomplish it, they will be able to do whatever they want, regardless of how challenging or terrifying it might be.

It's important to not make your child face the majority of their issues. If you press your child to much the child could end up with a result that is not what you'd like. It could create anxiety in the child and could lead to lasting effects. It could affect the self-esteem of children since the fear could hinder them from doing other tasks that they used to do easily.

Teach them to learn from THEIR MISTAKES

Since no one in the globe is perfect all of us make mistakes and errors at times. It is important that we grow as individuals and take lessons from our mistakes. Then, we must use these lessons to avoid repeating similar mistakes again in the future. This is all part of of maturation. It's the same with the child who wants to increase confidence in himself or herself.

The content in this chapter can assist you in teaching your child the importance of learning from mistakes and how this relates to self-confidence.

Help them learn

Your child has had more time in this world than you do. So it's only natural you're the one responsible for teaching your child how to take lessons from their mistakes. As an adult, you've probably had to go through this before and have more experience as compared to your son or daughter. Everyone has mistakes and nobody is perfect, as has been mentioned. What differentiates people who succeed from those who struggle is how much they can learn through their errors.

You can boost confidence in your child's self by achieving as well as it is possible for them to gain knowledge from their mistakes. If your child makes mistakes, you need to make sure they are not too harsh on themselves or be a victim to themselves. It is important to teach them to analyze the situation in a rational way and consider what they could do differently to obtain the best outcome. You'll be surprised by how this can boost the self-esteem of your child. This method will aid in making children's mental process develop and will help them gain confidence as they realize the fact that even when they fail to succeed in the first attempt they'll discover the cause then try again and eventually succeed.

If you don't show your child to take lessons from their mistakes confidence in themselves is likely to suffer. If your child doesn't learn from their mistakes, they is more likely to repeat the same mistakes. It can make children feel trapped in a rut or believe that it is impossible to succeed. They'll feel powerless to achieve any thing, so their drive to live will slowly diminish. Many people who are in prison regardless of age are a great example of this. If you inquire about the majority of people who are in the institution to answer a question, they'll most likely reply that no one instructed them on the value of making mistakes and learning from them. They continued to make identical mistakes, until eventually they became defeated and quit their efforts to succeed. This is something you would not wish to occur to your children. You should teach your child on the importance of learning from mistakes so that they can prevent a similar situation from happening.

Chapter 15: Self Confidence Strategy -"Look The Part

One of the most effective methods to boost confidence in yourself is to dress well. While confidence starts within, it is amplified by the clothes we put on. If you're confident then you're already on the way to becoming the top dawg or even an alpha male.

Before I show you how to dress properly, let me demonstrate why dressing properly is essential for building confidence in oneself and, ultimately becoming an Alpha.

The first impression that you make is hard to forget.

The first and most obvious advantage of dressing properly is to create an excellent impression on people generally and the hot woman you'd like to get acquainted with. I do not want to be like the majority of people, however, the appearance of a person does matter. No matter how much we push the concept of "don't evaluate a book based on its cover" in reality, we've always done. If you're not able to beat us, then join us!

This could be due to the way in which we as a species developed. In this Stone Age (not stoned age) humans did not enjoy the privilege of giving terrifying species like T-Rex or Raptor to benefit from the doubt "Oh it is surely a sweet cuddly creature in the inside, If allowed to!" Such naivete can result in being the night's dinner!

Unfortunately, this kind of thinking has been passed down from generation to generation , and it's become an evolutionary mechanism. Nowadays, however the risk is not in being torn in pieces, but being conned or being a victim of a very undesirable partner in a relationship that is exclusive!

If you're trying to become confident, you'll need some kind of social acceptance. In other words Without other people who aren't confident, you don't have any! In addition, without having other people to submit to your rule of law you won't have the chance to be a male alpha! This is like saying that you're the valedictorian in a class with one! Making a great first impression can make a huge difference in improving your self-confidence and eventually becoming an alpha.

Social Stand

No matter how many men claim that being assertive and alpha is only about being you, both of them requires good social standing. It's true that you cannot be considered the top dog when your the sole dog isn't it? Being on the top in the food chain of social interaction could boost your confidence than you've ever been. There is nothing that can more quickly make you the center of the minds of many people than dressing well.

CONTROL

If you're dressed well you can exercise control over a part of your life which can positively impact your personal achievement that in turn makes you feel more confident! Don't lie to me when you say that confidence is boosted when you are admired by others for your fashion sense. Yes, it happens. When you start receiving more compliments, it inspires you to put on a more professional appearance and boosts your confidence further to gigantic dimensions!

BRANDING

The truth is that the way you dress is the basis of how people view you. This can be beneficial or detrimental to confidence in yourself. Although you may feel confident in yourself If people constantly criticize the way you dress and feel, your confidence will diminish. If you dress professionally and confidently, your confidence will grow and increase to the size that of Shaquille O'Neal, or Yao Ming!

Suits make people believe you're a successful businessperson, the CEO, or a top lawyer. This is a great illustration of how your clothes will help you brand yourself in the best manner with others. When you dress properly, you're seen as confident and successful and an alpha male! In the event that you dress poorly, it portrays you as the man-bitch in your circle of friends.

AUTHORITIES AND INFLUENCE

Have you ever thought about why the best speakers - with the possible exception of extremely successful and wealthy people like Bill Gates and Steve Jobs and others - dress well all the time? Because dressing smartly could - at least in part make you appear more powerful over others. There's a difference between a personal finance professional with a nice crisp and crisp dress shirt tied into a nice set of pants, sporting Cole Haan sneakers and a classy blazer , and one wearing loose, round necked shirt and baggy pants with the pair of Chucks in shoes which do you think you'll show more respect and respect to? That's right - the Chucks guy!

HOW to dress smartly

Once you've realized the importance of dressing properly to boost confidence in yourself, let's talk about how you can achieve it. Start from scratch rather than simply altering your existing outfit. Why? You want your clothing to reflect who you wish to be - confident instead of having to adjust to your clothing. If your wardrobe is screaming "sissy!", there's no need to adapt to it, is it? If you don't want to be one, or remain one.

You can clearly saying "Objection Your Honor!", especially if you're over-budget. Don't worry, my padawan You don't have to complete everything in one shot! If you're able, that'd be wonderful, but if cannot, then take it in a time frame of a few weeks or even months if you have the funds. Just throw away the ugly of clothes items and purchase fresh ones, until you feel that the previous is completely gone and the new has arrived.

Assume that you know nothing

Let's face it, dude You're probably not sure or content with your style and that's the reason why you're reading this article. Recognizing this puts you in a great position to do something about it. I am proud of you!

Once I've established that, I'm also going to prove that what you're learning concerning fashion and fashion doesn't correspond to what you'd prefer to appear, and that implies that you know nothing or - I'll even be in the boldness of saying that you know nothing about dressing elegantly or professionally.

The best way to begin is to presume that you don't know anything about smart dress. It's simpler to learn to dress properly when you are aware of the basics, compared to knowing what that you thought was legitimate. It's like a canvas , it's much easier to make an original work on a clean one than one covered in the work of someone else.

If you've realized that you're really the basics of dressing properly You're now in a situation to seek assistance from others. There are three ways to accomplish this: employ an expert in fashion, request for a male friend who is fashionable to assist you in re-building your wardrobe, or conduct your own study.

The first choice is the most effective, however like most of the great items in the world it's likely to be the most expensive. If you're not engaged to or best friends with a stylist in order to receive the service at no cost. The reason this is the most effective is because professionals who are fashion consultants work for a living, and they aren't doing anything (or almost the same thing) for a living . They also remain up to date with the latest trends in fashion and the most lasting styles. It's similar to having an experienced manager of mutual funds to oversee your investments, or having a friend who is an occasional trading in the stock market as an interest.

The third option is advantageous, as you are somewhere in between employing a professional fashion consultant and conducting your own study. This gives you the advantage of having a second opinion on what looks good for the person you are (first advantage of this option) as well as the savings of doing it yourself at no cost (third alternative benefit). In terms of how you appear, it's ideal to have someone who has a good sense of the latest trends look at your. Everyone has blind spots, and until we've mastered dressing properly (what does work with us, and what isn't) We can't believe in our own opinion about how stylish and fashionable we look.

If you're not able to afford the expenses and you're hanging out mostly with the cast of The Big Bang Theory, you have no choice but to make things your own. The good news is that there's an abundance of information available on the Internet and in the printed media (books or magazines, etc.). This is because it doesn't offer you an impartial outsider's assessment of the style you're considering It's best to use this as an option last resort.

STICK to THE BASICS

The most effective way to look great, particularly those who aren't comfortable with it adhere to the basic rules. With these, you will not be disappointed. If you master the basics right, you'll be nearly seventy percent accomplished with your personal style. This can navigate through the most social occasions without any issues and with a newfound confidence.

What are the fundamentals that you should know? These are the clothes that can help you look great for the social situations you might encounter. This includes white round neck tshirts, dark blue jeans with the dark navy blue blazer and decent pair of shoes and loafers. These items of clothing aren't just suitable for most social settings but they also function as your own personal style education base as you work on learning the basics and, eventually developing your individual style signature. Be careful not to succumb to the urge to add accessories make sure you only do this once you've got the basics down.

Simple AND SAVING

Men often think they can learn from women with regards to their personal style. i.e. they'll appear attractive with a variety of accessories, and wear an extravagant style. This is a women"thank you, dawg! This isn't the case for us self-confident, alpha folks and it's all about simplicity elegance. A famous, but also deceased - alpha male once stated simple is the most sophisticated of all.

Keep it simple, but stylish. Confidence is about not having to be a slouch. If you try too hard, it's insecurity and a strong desire to be loved by others that are the exact opposite of the confident male.

You can't look good If YA'S FIT OFF

There's an Ten Commandments for dressing well that's the equivalent to "thou will not be a slave to any gods other than me" which is the most important order, is this you should not try to squeeze yourself into clothes that are too loose or tight! Do not fret if you've got the body and face of the two most famous Ryans on the planet that is Ryan Reynolds and Ryan Gosling. If you're wearing shirts or pants that are at least two sizes smaller, you'll achieve looking as strong male like Richard Simmons - I smell something burning...it is probably your weight! If you're wearing clothes at least 2 sizes larger and you'll only be able to achieve appearing as powerful like Alvin as well as the Chipmunks. Only a handful of males (mostly hip-hoppers) are able to pull off the look such as, for instance Snoop Dogg or Jay-Z.

What exactly is the best suit for you? For shirts, the main indication will be the line that runs across your shoulders. Both lines should sit on the shoulders' edges but not prior to or after. If they are ahead of the shoulders' edges, you'll notice that it's tight. If it's later it's loose.

Another way to determine whether your shirt is long is by how it appears when you're not tucked in. When the western edge extends over your crotch the shirt is too long. If it's higher the crotch, it's too short.

For your pants and pants. The best method to test it at the mirror is when you appear as if you're at a hip-hop festival or look like MC Hammer in a suit and tie. You know that you're wearing loose pants bro. In case your crown jewels seem to be getting too tight together to the point where your voice sounds similar to Mike Tyson after being hit with a ball then you're sure the pants aren't tight. Choose a middle-of-the-road feeling.

JUST enough

If you're a bit overloaded with clothes, it's as annoying as having too many. Being aware of this, establishing an eye on your budget for outfit overhaul should be an absolute joy! Trust me when I say that the more you spend, the less. It's just like drinking alcohol - it becomes really bad after the point at which it becomes a problem. However, instead of throwing up and suffering a horrible hangover, being too heavy on your clothes could cause the pockets of your wallet, and cause you suffer from paralysis of the wardrobe.

A good way to go about this is to regularly look through your closet for items that don't fit properly anymore (loose or snug, what ever) or have worn in color. Get rid of them so that your closet will have more space or you'll have room to put in better fitting and attractive ones in the future.

DIVERSITY IS VERY COMFY

In the end, good looks will make you feel confident, but wearing the same clothes over and over again will reduce the confidence. What if Jake Gyllenhaal wearing the same pants and shirt all day long for one month? His status as an Alpha male could drop, even if only a little did it. As there's no Jake Gyllenhaal in your life wearing the same outfit every day can cause significant alpha male as well as confidence issues. This is why it's crucial to change your clothing appearances.

It is important to understand that the word "variation" doesn't refer to quantity. It's all about various styles or colors. It's about having more than a handful of white t-shirts, but also others in different designs and colors. Keep in mind that you should include enough variety into a wardrobe that is ideal size (remember that you only need a little?). When it comes to shoes you'll be fine with three pairs that are formal, casual and athletic.

Chapter 16: Effective Strategies To Ensure Success

Some people are confident about things but never attempt them. You might be convinced that you'll be an excellent low-level manager but you'll never try it because you think that you don't have anything to demonstrate.

A person who is confident will do things that really test them. More importantly, they will do things that can inspire them.

However, we must be real. Before you begin writing the next best-selling book in the world or even set your sights at being the first person to walk on Saturn it is important to take the little steps to make sure you're as comfortable and content as you're able to be.

Check out this list. The majority of the information is common sense, but it's not widely used.

1. Smiley Face -- Yes it's an actual smile. It's not an emoticon. It's it's a smile. Studies have

shown that smiling in stressful times can lower heart rate and increase positive emotions. Physical movement can make you feel more peaceful and comfortable. It stimulates neurotransmitters within the brain. Do it!

2. Kind Acts: Volunteer somewhere. Send baked goods or a thank-you note or a wish-for-well card and wish someone an happy birthday, open the door, cook someone dinner, you know the concept. It's important to remember that when you assist others, you realize the power of your actions and have the ability to make a difference in some way or another. Think of people as generally decent and strive to enhance this positive. You'll feel more satisfied and more assured. It's too short to waste time with other people. Do not waste time pondering negative thoughts. Go out and share the good.

3. People with low self-esteem will dismiss compliments or even ignore them completely. Certain people may see there is a motive behind harmless compliments.

Stop! You can feel good knowing that someone is interested enough to speak up. Most people mean it. If you're feeling down, take a moment to remember the praises and pull your self back.

What do you think? Someone is grateful to you!

4. Dress Well--This doesn't mean that you must wear a costly gown or suit. This means wearing something you love, and that shows that you are who you are. Make yourself look cool. Be cool, stylish, spunky and slick. Be nerdy, slick, hippie, goofy and comfy. yourself. Be yourself and love the clothes you're in.

5. Exercise--Sick of hearing this? It's real! Exercise boosts your mood, reduces stressand can transform your perspective about your life. It is possible to discuss specific neural compounds or the loss of weight or muscle The bottom line is that It's good for you!

It doesn't matter if you're running a marathon or be a competitive cross-fitter. Try to do 20-30 minutes whenever you are able to. Don't think you don't have the time. If you are unable to spare 20 minutes every few days then you should unwind and take a break from committing so much time to other activities. Be aware that this is your life. Your life.

6. Good Posture: Sound absurd? Actually, studies suggest differently. Slouching is seen as negative and can also affect your posture in time. Keep your body straight and relaxed shoulders. Keep your chin in the air and your eyes open. It will make you feel confident. You'll appear more confident, and experience improved breathing and a stronger core. Stand tall and do not slide.

7. Good Food is another obvious option. All the time, fast food will leave you feeling physically and mentally tired. A diet that is not healthy can result in health issues and depression. Cooking a tasty dinner is easier and more pleasant than many people imagine. Many people say not having time or energy, however this isn't true. Google "quick simple healthy meals" and enjoy the meal! You might uncover the culinary skills you didn't realize you already had.

8. Smile and tell yourself that the majority of people are decent people, and that If you treat them as you would like to be treated and they will, as a result behave in the manner you would like to be treated. Do you think that's easy enough?

Furthermore what is the reason you would assume that people don't like you? Are you really so bad? Do you think everyone else is obsessed with your perceived flaws and shortcomings? What do you consider?

Most people are caught up in their own worries and thoughts to be concerned about theirs. Be friendly, believe you're nice to people and stop worrying about them. You'll be amazed at how nice individuals can be if you treat them well.

9. Organization--Set your priorities straight. This isn't about getting clean and tidy. I'm simply suggesting that organizing your material and non-materials (thoughts emotions, feelings, thoughts) are able to do wonderful things for you.

Make sure you organize things in a way that you can manage. Don't get overwhelmed. Find your way and take it in stride.

10.Meditation--Many people believe that meditation is just a bunch of b.s. Meditation can help reduce stress, relaxation, and efficiency. It can also help with depression blood pressure, depression, and heart diseases. The strength of the brain, as measured by the amount of gyrification or the folding of the brain's tissue, is improved by meditation. Also, you can meditate, and view things with greater clarity!

11.Me-Time--Make me-time a priority especially if you've been through stress-inducing moments. Find ways to be kind to yourself and not scold yourself for the occasional lapses. It's okay to be human and cry out loud!

Sometimes, you can plan an evening of movies, an evening out, or a addictive pleasure. Enjoy a relaxing, warm bath. Enjoy a fine liqueur. Keep in mind that part of living life is to enjoy pleasure. It doesn't mean that we need to do anything illegal and behave a bit "naughty" from time moment is completely acceptable.

12.Mirror Mind--Remove your eyes from the mirror. If you're not practicing eye contact or performing funny impressions it's probably not a good idea to spend so much time looking into the mirror. Studies show that frequent "mirror-gazing can increase self-esteem issues. It's one thing to appear attractive prior to going out in public. It's quite another to be so absorbed in looking 'spruced-up' and then never get out.

13.Test Yourself. That's right, test yourself. time. You are in a new scenario. Speak to strangers. Participate in a contest or go to an event or read a novel or start an exciting new pastime. The key is you must push yourself and learn to overcome challenges. If you are able to push yourself and persist, you will succeed. Don't allow fear to get in your way. Show yourself that you are the most powerful person you are.

Take a step back from the couch and get out of your home comfort zone!

There are plenty of possibilities for people to blossom. It is possible to take small daily steps that are essential to building confidence in ourselves and becoming more healthy more content, happier and stronger. Confidence can be found in all aspects within our daily lives. We all can do it.

However, sometimes we need additional assistance. Sometimes, in spite of every piece of advice and every ounce of experience, we be unable to overcome the challenges.

Sometimes, in the quest to conquer life, it is necessary to need to be able to conquer our emotions. The only way to conquer our emotions must be to let them come to the surface.

We can't hide our emotions. It is possible to think that we can keep them from us as they aren't able to harm us.

However, they'll. They'll rise and explode, they'll wreak havoc on our bodies and minds until the end of the day. If we attempt to shut down our emotions, we're only harming ourselves.

If we don't confront them, we'll never get them fixed...

Chapter 17: The Common Roots Of Low Self-Esteem

Self-esteem issues can be triggered when we are children. We are exposed to a variety about ourselves from parents as well as our siblings, colleagues, our friends and the media. The information we receive is both negative and positive and yet in some way, the negative information is typically the one we will remember the most.

At a very young age, we are conditioned to follow certain rules and act in the way we want to (to behave in a certain way) and we are also expected to set the expectations of our own on ourselves. We often do not think we're able to be able to meet the standards of other people or our own expectations for that matter.

Being in a tough spot in your life (also how you see your life) along with anxiety and even a severe illness can impact on self-esteem.

It's a well-known fact that certain people tend to be more focused on negative aspects than positive. There are people who set high standards for themselves that they fail to live up to them.

It is, therefore, crucial to understand what the symptoms and signs are so that you are capable of identifying when they are having a problem, and can work to improve confidence in yourself.

It is equally important to understand what the primary reason behind your self-esteem issues is. There are a variety of factors that could affect your self-esteem, like:

* Feeling lonely

* Being unemployed

Feeling left out

Feeling lonely

Feeling like being an "outcast"

* Being abused

Feelings of low performance

How to Increase Self-Esteem and Improve Low Self-Esteem

To boost confidence in yourself, you have to be able recognize the negative thoughts about yourself. You must ask yourself the reasons behind those opinions (where did you acquire them) or from where the origins of them came from.

The most effective method to combat this is to record your negative beliefs about yourself. Then, be aware and actively collect evidence that contradicts these negative beliefs. That is, counter the negative beliefs with positive ones. (Write down your positive beliefs as well).

Be aware of any negative thoughts that pop up in your mind. Ask yourself what the reason was and when it started. Write them down in a journal. the details down.

Also, take note of evidence to counter those negative beliefs. You can counter them with positive ones. Write them down within your diary.

Find five things you think you're great in or that you believe are true about yourself (this might be something people have praised you on).

Write down the five positive qualities and place it in a spot somewhere that it is easy to you so to serve to remind you on a regular basis that you're capable of things and that you're worthy of it!

Simple Steps to Increase Self-Esteem and Self-esteem

Do not try to compare yourself with other people.

Concentrate on the things you can change

*Do things that you're interested in or find enjoyable

*Live your life in gratitude

Be positive (and talk positively to yourself)

Maintain a healthy lifestyle and work out

Don't worry about perfection

*Be less critical of you (when you make errors)

*Live your life with a sense compassion and empathy

Surround yourself with people who are supportive and love you

Don't compare yourself to other people.

It is not a good idea to look at yourself in comparison to others as you are unique with your own talents. One of the biggest mistakes individuals make is try to compare themselves to other people. But, it is the fastest method by which you will be able to see any flaws that you feel you are lacking. If you don't compare to others, you'll not feel the requirement to take on competition.

Look at what you can change

Make sure you focus on things you can control, and not worry about things that are beyond your control. A lot of people worry about things that they are not in control of and cause them to stress themselves out. If you can shift your focus on the positive, you'll experience an optimistic perspective.

Do activities that you're passionate about or something you love.

Find more things you're enthusiastic about or truly love. We tend to give priority to the other responsibilities in our lives, instead of finding time to do things that is something we truly love. When we are doing something that we love it gives us a general sense of happiness.

Be grateful and live your life

Feel grateful and take time to be grateful for what that you've got, because gratitude will bring more abundance since you'll notice many things happening in your world that you should be thankful for. Happiness and joy are the result of gratitude. can be described as emotional health.

Be positive (and talk positively to yourself)

Maintain an optimistic view of your life and yourself. It is very easy to be entangled in a negative mindset or thinking pattern. Be sure to notice your positive qualities and give yourself a compliment. Talk to yourself the way you would speak to your friend you love the most.

Maintain a healthy lifestyle and get active

Make an effort to lead a healthier lifestyle , and incorporate exercises. Life has become so hectic that many do not put in the time or time into eating healthy meals or meals. Take a look at the long-term effects that eating healthy and exercise can be able to have on the body... Your body is going to be grateful for it.

Don't worry about perfection

Do not try that is perfect. If we try to achieve perfection, we open ourselves in the position of failing, since there is no way to be flawless. Instead, try to be the best you can achieve.

Don't be so critical of your self (when you make errors)

Do not be a shambles for making mistakes. Many people make mistakes because it is human nature. But, think about this alternatively... Without mistakes there is no learning and there is no room for improvement.

Be a person who has a sense of compassion and empathy

Be able to live your life with an understanding of empathy and compassion. Sometimes it's easy to let someone down and then bury the heads "in the sand" (in your personal life). However, when we show compassion toward others or assist people who is in need, we benefit ourselves.

Be surrounded by people who are supportive and love you.

Make sure you surround yourself with positive people and those who are supportive and love you. We often spend our time with the wrong people. People who hurt us, instead of helping us grow. Be around people who make you feel happy as well as loved and respected.

Additional Methods to Enhance Low Self-Esteem

There are many ways we can boost self-esteem and improve self-esteem. In addition to the methods previously mentioned, you can consider the following options:

* Be gentle with yourself

* Develop assertiveness

Recognize your strengths

* Establish positive relationships

• Learn how to use the word "no"

* Set goals for yourself

Be Kind to Youself

So, try to be kind to yourself. Make time to read a great book, sit down to watch a great film, take a walk in the outdoors or doing something you truly enjoy.

If you find yourself being harsh on yourself, imagine what you would tell your friend who you love dearly and you'll find you'd probably never be so harsh.

The manner in which we talk to our most trusted friend is typically gentle and affectionate, while the suggestions we give to a friend is typically less important than the advice we give to ourselves.

Learn to be confident and assertive

Being assertive does not suggest that we are offended by the views of others. Be yourself and be able to express your thoughts in a respectful manner (without inflicting any offense on others).

It is important to be honest and open about your feelings, thoughts and opinions, and share these with others. You'll soon discover that they won't need to be offended but instead appreciate your honesty and openness rather.

Being assertive can also give you a sense that you are free and confidence, since you'll be able to communicate your feelings and be open with other people.

Recognize Your Strengths

Everyone has an ability, a skill or something we excel at such as telling short stories or poetry writing or singing, playing guitar or cooking or even creating puzzles.

We tend to appreciate the things we excel at and this gives us an inner satisfaction and inner happiness. Also, we have a sense of obligation to utilize these abilities to the very highest of our abilities.

Once you've discovered your talent or gift take the initiative to use it the best job feasible and you'll soon realize that this brings happiness and peace into your life.

Establish Positive Relations

Sometimes, people who are negative are in our paths and we might allow that individuals into our lives. However, they can also bring one down.

Do not allow these people to enter your personal life in order for them don't have a positive impact on us. Focus on connecting with positive people, who seek to inspire others.

Focus on spending time with those who love your well-being, who appreciate you , and are optimistic about life. They always make the most of the others.

You can learn to say "No"

Conclusion

I'm sure by now you've come to the conclusion that you do not have to be worried about or apologize for being confident in the event that you're regularly smug about your abilities or exhibit narcissistic traits but these do not prove that you're confident in yourself. There are many advantages from displaying confidence, with some helping you become an effective leader within the organization you could be involved in as you're less anxious or stressed and also gaining confidence in yourself to achieve the goals you've been putting off for years to achieve, just to name some. It's not only the advantages you must focus on, but for some time there is immense worth recognizing the positive results that occur when you become an incredibly confident person It is also important to acknowledge every point of view from psychologists who share their views on the issue and also. While they are valid, they shouldn't be considered as mere facets of a larger truth However, they could give some insight into what triggers people to be more confident in themselves which could or won't correspond to the current circumstances within your own life. Additionally, they are intended to broaden your perception of self-confidence, if you are also taking the time to research what strategies to aid you in becoming more confident are most beneficial for you. Some of them are more simple in nature, while others are more sophisticated.

www.ingramcontent.com/pod-product-compliance
Lightning Source LLC
Chambersburg PA
CBHW071840080526
44589CB00012B/1066